New

Directions in

Latin American

Architecture

NEW DIRECTIONS IN ARCHITECTURE

NEW DIRECTIONS IN LATIN AMERICAN ARCHITECTURE
by Francisco Bullrich

NEW DIRECTIONS IN AFRICAN ARCHITECTURE
by Udo Kultermann

NEW DIRECTIONS IN AMERICAN ARCHITECTURE
by Robert A. M. Stern

NEW DIRECTIONS IN BRITISH ARCHITECTURE
by Royston Landau

NEW DIRECTIONS IN GERMAN ARCHITECTURE
by Günther Feuerstein

NEW DIRECTIONS IN ITALIAN ARCHITECTURE
by Vittorio Gregotti

NEW DIRECTIONS IN JAPANESE ARCHITECTURE
by Robin Boyd

NEW DIRECTIONS IN SOVIET ARCHITECTURE
by Anatole Kopp

NEW DIRECTIONS IN SWISS ARCHITECTURE
by Jul Bachmann and Stanislaus von Moos

FRANCISCO BULLRICH

NEW DIRECTIONS

IN

LATIN AMERICAN

ARCHITECTURE

GEORGE BRAZILLER   NEW YORK

To the memory of Alicia, my wife

CONTENTS

Foreword   *11*

PAST AND PRESENT   *13*

BRAZIL   *22*

MEXICO   *28*

ARGENTINA   *30*

URBAN UTOPIA AND REALITY   *35*

TOWNSCAPE ARCHITECTURE   *49*

TECHNOLOGY AND ARCHITECTURE   *54*

CARLOS RAÚL VILLANUEVA   *73*

MONUMENTAL ARCHITECTURE   *83*

THE NEW GENERATION   *93*

Notes   *119*

Bibliography   *121*

Index   *123*

Sources of Illustrations   *128*

FOREWORD

This book is offered as an interim account of architecture in Latin America today. The reader will understand, I am sure, the difficulty of compressing the vast material implied by the scope of the subject into a volume of limited dimensions. I could have attempted a highly brief survey of each of the twenty Latin American nations, but this would have resulted in little more than an illustrated catalogue. On the other hand, a select treatment of a few countries, such as Brazil, Mexico, and Argentina, would have resulted in serious omissions and given a distorted view. I chose, therefore, to present the architects and their works, not according to their nationality, but in relation to the problems which are now being confronted in this area of the world. Yet national features are important and should not be entirely sacrificed. Thus, wherever the opportunity arose, I referred to national development in order to give the reader at least a capsule image of a country's architectural characteristics.

Although I had intended to deal almost exclusively with current developments, I felt that a review of the recent past was necessary for a proper understanding of the present. This has inevitably led to discussions of older, established architects and their most significant works—especially as these projects have touched on questions of concern today.

No one can presume to possess a detailed and up to the minute knowledge of every current development in architecture throughout Latin America. And while I have traveled the continent extensively, I have had to rely on periodicals when firsthand information was not available. It is possible that a very recent and interesting project may have been omitted; nevertheless, every effort has been made to make this book a reasonably complete and accurate image of the subject.

Finally, I want to thank the architects mentioned in the book who sent me the material necessary for its presentation, and Mrs. Virginia G. de Jaxa Debicki, Mrs. Maria T. de Dellepiane, Mrs. Lala Mendez Mosquera, Professor Aurelio Lucchini, and the architects Max Cetto, Roberto Segre, Jorge E. Hardoy, and Antonio Diaz for their help.

Francisco Bullrich
Buenos Aires, December, 1968

PAST AND PRESENT

WHEN World War II came to an end, critics and editors of architectural journals throughout the world suddenly realized that important changes in architecture had been taking place in Brazil since 1938. Later, attention was drawn to Venezuela and Mexico as well as to other nations of Latin America. It is often assumed that in architecture, as in other fields, developments in every country arose from an identical set of circumstances, and that what was true for one country was true for all. This assumption, however, ignores the differences which Latin America's continental dimensions and cultural differences inevitably imply. Although the socioeconomic conditions and the cultural evolution of these countries have much in common, they are not interchangeable. Nor are the architectural traditions fully identical, and this fact accounts for the differences we may find in the work of present day architects.

A world of difference separates the evolution of the great Central American cultures from those which developed in the rarified climate of the Bolivian high plateau or along the Pacific coast of Peru. Although we may admire the vigor of their stone sculptures and the refinement of their pottery designs, the cultures of northwest Argentina never produced a work which attained the monumental quality of the fortress Sacsahuaman in Peru, or the urbanistic elaboration of Chichén-Itzá in Mexico. There is almost nothing in common between the Incas and the tribes that confronted the immensity of the Pampa horizons or the wildness of the Amazonic Mato.

That is why Latin Americans themselves look upon their pre-Columbian past in different ways. It is, for example, very difficult for an Argentine to accept as his own heritage that which he never experiences in an immediate way. On the other hand, a Mexican is continually confronted with reminders that once Tezcatlipoca, the "smoking mirror," reigned over the four cardinal points, projecting himself in each with a different color. Every day at dawn the fishermen on Lake Titicaca go out to work with tools and canoes that were designed many thousands of years ago. Although they might have a little village with a plaza and a chapel nearby, they do not seem touched by historical evolution in either their lives or their surroundings. Their experience has almost no relationship whatever to that of the people living in the great centers of Latin America.

From the walls of Machu-Pichu, a descendant of the Incas may gaze at the mountains in the distance, but he does not seem to perceive much more of this past than we do. Did the Spanish conquest thus forever preclude an understanding of a world lighted by sun myths? And yet, as if driven by a metaphysical anguish, Latin Americans look back at the powerful walls of Cuzco and discover in the tense arrangement of the masonry an outlook and feeling which they believe should be theirs.

All explanations of this phenomenon must take into account that Latin America is a heritage of the Spanish conquest. It is not always understood that Spain is many different things—at once Narcisco Tomé's loquacious, colorful *Trasparente* and the austere grandiosity of El Escorial. One must also realize that the Portuguese and Spanish traditions were not identical. Although at one time both countries were governed by the same monarch, Philip II (reigned 1556–98), the urban layout of the Brazilian cities such as Bahia or Ouro Preto reflect very clearly the looser governmental attitude toward the building of these cities than toward the equivalent Spanish colonial ones. The authoritarian grid-iron system apparently was applied almost universally in Spanish America, and only a few cities seem to have escaped it. Although the Spanish conquest meant the almost total obliteration of pre-existing urban cultures, the new centers of power often rose dramatically above the ruins of old walls, giving a surprising historical continuity.[1]

The violent cultural clash resulting from this conquest took different forms and had different effects in the diverse areas of Latin America, varying according to the strength of the preceding Indian cultures. Bolivia, Mexico, and Peru can claim a great architectural colonial past, in which the artistic tendencies of the European colonizers were integrated with the native craftsmen's needs for expression (or with the Africans' experience, as in the case of Brazil). But there is nothing in Uruguay or Chile that can be compared to Peru's Plaza del Cuzco, or to the Sagrario chapel of Puebla, Mexico. In fact, the quality of most colonial architecture is more spontaneous and popular than refined or traditional.

The colonial cities differed distinctly from those in their mother countries. "While the city of Western Europe represented a movement of economic energies away from extractive pursuits towards those of processing and distribution, the Latin American city was the core of energy and organization for exploitation of natural resources."[2] Thus while the European city evolved centripetally the Latin American city evolved centrifugally.

The political independence won in the early nineteenth century spelled the end of the colonial tradition in Latin America. This process varied in intensity and significance. The Rio de la Plata region went through a period of extreme Europeanization and cosmopolitanism, especially during the second half of the century. Here the massive immigration of Spaniards, Italians, English, and French decisively altered the ethnic and cultural structure of the population. This situation was not duplicated in Mexico or Brazil, even though these countries also show signs of the same evolution. Ruling classes of the southern nations (Chile, Argentina, and Uruguay) managed to eradicate the old cultural patterns and substitute them with new ones imported from Europe; but elsewhere this attempt failed. In Mexico native tradition prevailed, and political reaction resisted first French intervention and then *Porfirismo*.[3] In Brazil popular tradition also survived because the upper classes, strangely enough, maintained the patterns of plantation culture for a long time, and never tried to oppose the African folkways of the greater part of the population. One needs only a superficial knowledge of South American cities to perceive their profound differences, which express the diverse cultural experiences of each country.

In Mexico City the colonial past is a powerful background, and, although it is often rejected at the level of social consciousness, it continues to control the extended historical conflict, the attitudes, the spiritual reality, the town and landscape. On the other hand, Buenos Aires nearly lacks colonial architecture, and most of the city center looks very much like Paris and London. By 1880 stylistic revivals of Italian Renaissance and French *dix-huitième* were flourishing. Such revivals implied a loss of national authenticity, since they meant a deceitful nostalgia for the past of others. Art Nouveau arrived in the early twentieth century but was considered of bad taste almost everywhere. Perhaps the most monumental work of the period is in a way a mixture of neobaroque and Art Nouveau: the Palacio de Bellas Artes in Mexico City, originally the Teatro Nacional (begun in 1904 by Adamo Boari, an Italian, and completed in 1934 by Federíco Mariscal).

Julián García Nuñez (1875–1944) was probably the most outstanding Latin American architect of the time who consistently developed a genuine language. He studied in Barcelona under Antonio Gaudí and Domenech y Montaner, and returned to Buenos Aires, his birthplace, where among other works he built the Hospital Español in 1908 (*Figs. 1–2*). Today his architecture, more inclined toward the rigid forms of Sezessionstil than to the looser grammar of Catalanism, is regarded as an important precedent, after having been ignored for many years.

Reaction against dependence on French and English precedents began to rise early in the 1910's, but it led to a position equally remote from the crucial architectural movements of the day—a Spanish and colonial revival. Such an anachronism could not resolve the urgent search for an authentic national expression.

But from the beginning of the century architects began concentrating on Latin American architecture, first in general and then on that of individual nations. In Argentina, Alejandro Christophersen, of Norwegian descent, proposed to discard the French *dix-huitième* pastiche and to explore new directions inspired by the traditions of the country, thus creating an art that would reflect in every detail the climate, morals, and building materials of Argentina.[4]

Years later, Lúcio Costa and his young companions, who led the modern movement in Brazil, attempted to adapt the vocabulary of modern architecture to the tropical environment, such as the sun's heat and glare. They also sought some kind of relationship between the forms and procedures of the great architectural past and contemporary architecture. The former effort led to the introduction of *brise-soleils*, or sunbreakers, the latter to, on the one hand, the use of *azuleijos* (painted ceramic tiles) and to, on the other,

1. *Julián Garcia Nuñez: Hospital Español, Buenos Aires, Argentina, 1908.*

looser forms which recalled the Brazilian baroque architecture of the late eighteenth century. Almost the same trend took place in Mexico in the fifties, when the crude functionalism of José Villagrán García was followed by a revival of pre-Columbian forms.

That the problem of national architecture is debated is sufficient proof in itself that Latin American architects are conscious of their dependence on European and North American models; this awareness is part of Latin America's struggle to achieve a new, defined cultural personality. It is necessary to analyze the true nature of this problem and to eliminate some of the ambiguities that have often been brought into the discussion. It is repeatedly assumed that the mere transcription of some objective regional facts is equivalent to

2. *Hospital Español, interior.*

an authentic artistic expression. It is also assumed that there exists something such as a constituted national entity whose distinctive expression must be revealed. However, transcribing objectivity has never produced a genuine work of art. And it has been impossible to discover such a thing as an a priori national essence which is expressed artistically ex post facto. If a national spirit, or *Volkgeist*, does exist, it is not a historical constant, but a variable, not an impersonal force but a quality residing in the individual. It is the single work of art that contributes to bringing into being such a concept as a national spirit. In trying to justify irrationalism as conforming to the eternal Aztec racial instinct, Mexican architects often refer to Alois Riegl's and Wilhelm Worringer's ideas. But it is rather difficult to believe that either a *Kunstwollen* (collective will to form) or a *Volkgeist* is the result of a biological heritage, even if these abstractions should exist as more than instruments of critical generalization. The hispanicism of Spanish art, for example, cannot exist independently of the work of such men as Diego Velazquez, the Churriguera family, Juan de Herrera, Antonio Gaudí, or the creators of anonymous popular architecture. On the contrary, it is a reality which emerges out of their own works and which wins universal recognition only because these works have superseded the simple local dialect and have spoken a universal language. In Latin America, political nationalism has played an important role in the formation of artistic ideas by always assuming that all contacts with Europe inevitably lead to alien and, therefore, unauthentic expressions. It might be affirmed, however, that the unauthenticity of the so-called non-American expression does not fundamentally lie, as nationalism believes, in the ethical-political field, but rather in the strict field of art itself. What condemns the so-called non-American expression is its lack of artistic authenticity. National expression, therefore, will never be the result of programming or of theoretical preconceptions, as these measures can only lead to clichés; it cannot and will not be a self-imposed product, but the result of a genuine creative process.

One can understand the relationship between the process of national expression and modern architecture by looking at the origins of modern architecture in Latin America. Rationalism appeared in the hispano-american world in the twenties as a cultural import. It is true that functionalism was a new source of inspiration that freed architects' imaginations from sterile stylistic formulas and engaged its followers in a sincere search for a new architectural expression based on an objective evaluation of modern man's needs and on the new technical means at his disposal. But the local socioeconomic and cultural circumstances differed from those in Europe at the time. Inevitably, the first rationalistic attempts were more expressions of a progressive, isolated *inteligenzia* rather than products solidly rooted in Latin American soil. These efforts did not enjoy popularity, as the so-called upper classes did not favor them, and the masses could not understand the ascetic vocabulary. Although this situation severely limited the possible architectural scope, many important works were executed between 1928 and 1938 which may be considered antecedents of later work.

José Villagrán García, Juan O'Gorman, and Max Cetto in Mexico, Gregori Warchavchik and Alvaro Vital in Brazil, Julio Vilamajó and Oscar Cravotto in Uruguay, A. U. Vilar and Alberto Prebisch in Argentina, all put special emphasis on internationalism and considered localism regressive. O'Gorman's house at Villa Obregón, Mexico (1929), Villagrán's house in Calle Dublin, Mexico City (1937), like Vilamajó's house in Montevideo (1930), or Warchavchik's house in Rua Itápolis, São Paulo (1928), might have been built anywhere in the world. The attitude of these men conceals a flagrant contradiction. If function constitutes the basis of all forms, why should not architectural works somehow reflect differences in climate, social conditions, and technical procedures? Functionalism by its very definition could lead only to a regionalistic diversification, as it eventually did not only in the Latin American countries but also in the rest of the world. Reaction against the attitude of abstract functionalism started within the vanguard of European movements. The interest in typical forms of folk construction and the birth of Scandinavian neoempiricism began around 1940.

The Latin American counterparts included: in Brazil the new movement, headed by Lúcio Costa, that began with the Ministry of

3. *Julio Vilamajó: Facultad de Ingeniería, Montevideo, Uruguay, 1938.*

Education and Health building in Rio de Janeiro (1937–43); in Mexico the pre-Columbian revival which started around 1950; and in Argentina the "Austral" (southern) movement. The significance of these three trends, apart from their common reaction against the *machine à habiter*, and their concern with the social aspects of architecture and urbanism, was considerable. Their pioneering action, along with that of Julio Vilamajó in Uruguay and Carlos Raúl Villanueva in Venezuela, opened the way to present-day experience and must be considered in order to understand the new directions in Latin American architecture.

The theories of Julio Vilamajó (1894–1948), the most independent personality practicing in Latin America during the thirties, profoundly influenced architects in both Uruguay and Argentina. His empirical attitude, his indifference to international style clichés, his concern

4. *Julio Vilamajó: Private house, Montevideo, Uruguay, 1930.*

with psychological aspects of architectural experience, and his sensitivity to spatial relationships made him in many ways equivalent to Gunnar Asplund.

His works, which at first reflected the romantic trend of classical simplification (*Figs. 3–4*), acquired a definite neoempirical accent by the early forties, as for instance in the hostels and houses of Villa Serrana in Uruguay (*Fig. 5*). Although in the mid- and late forties his works were looked upon by the younger Rio de la Plata generation, especially the Austral group, as a retreat from modern architecture, they later drew more attention after the polemics had died down and some of the practicalities and limitations of the building techniques had begun to be considered as a "given" or "starting" element. Vilamajó has thus become one of the seminal masters of Uruguayan architecture.

5. *Julio Vilamajó: Ventorrillo, Villa Serrana, Minas, Uruguay, 1943.*

BRAZIL

THE Ministry of Education and Health building in Rio de Janeiro (*Fig. 6*), by Lúcio Costa, Oscar Niemeyer, and others in consultation with Le Corbusier, is generally considered the starting point of the Brazilian development which later became world famous. Although it is certainly the first modern masterpiece in Brazil, it was preceded by a number of noteworthy achievements, such as the Hostel for the Homeless by Eduardo Affonso Reidy (Rio de Janeiro, 1933), the first Santos Dumont airport building by Atilio Correia Lima (Rio de Janeiro, 1937), and the plaza in Recife by Roberto Burle Marx (1935). All show that enough local activity already existed to enable a real dialogue to take place when Le Corbusier came to Rio de Janeiro in 1936 as a consultant to the Brazilian team. This assertion is not intended to diminish Le Corbusier's influence, which was decisive both for the design of the Ministry building itself and for the evolution of the Brazilian movement as a whole.

The Ministry building was, in itself, a manifesto of the new architecture in Brazil. On the one hand it very clearly reflects Le Corbusier's ideas: the building raised on free-standing *pilotis*, the independent structure, the free plan, the *pan de verre* as an ideal limit of the inner space, the building as an isolated volume in urban space, the continuity at ground level, and so forth. On the other hand, the use of *azuleijos* and *brise-soleils*, with the use of tropical flora (which had been almost ignored until then) in the gardens which designed by Roberto Burle Marx in the plaza facing the building and in the upper terraces, were evidence of the building's regionalistic intention.

The continuity between inner and outer space, one of the basic tenets of modern architecture, found in Brazil its ideal homeland. Through modernism, Brazilian architecture could thus recover a characteristic that had been common in the old plantation houses and had been lost with Beaux-Arts academicism, which had tried to ignore the tropical environment. The curving contours, which later became a typical feature of the modern Brazilian vernacular, first appeared in the Ministry building in the design of the water tanks at the top, in the disposition of the flower beds in the gardens, and in the lazy lineal designs of Candido Portinari's mosaics.

The whole scheme is visibly an attempt at the integration of art, architecture, urbanism, and landscaping. Sociopolitical commitment is apparent in Portinari's large paintings in the minister's office.

Le Corbusier's activity in Brazil was not limited to working with a select group of architects. Through a number of lectures he came into contact with a wider audience composed mainly of officials of the *Estado Novo*,[5] as well as of connoisseurs. This helps explain how the new movement could grow under the wing of the State and become the official architecture of Brazil.

Brazilian architecture is not a one-track process. While Lúcio Costa returned to folklike architecture in the hostel at Nova Friburgo (1944) and the Hungria Machado House (Rio de Janeiro, 1942) where he used the traditional *muxarabis* (wooden shutters) instead of *brise-*

6. *Lúcio Costa, Oscar Niemeyer, and others, in consultation with Le Corbusier: Ministry of Education and Health, Rio de Janeiro, Brazil, 1938–43.*

soleils, Oscar Niemeyer evolved a very loose approach in his Casa do Baile (*Fig. 7*). Although this work might be related to some of Le Corbusier's, and to an attempted revival of the Brazilian baroque, it clearly re-creates the forms of tropical flora. It also expresses an exuberant rhythm and movement obviously inspired by the Afro-Brazilian dancing it houses. It seems as though there are echoes of the poised movements of the *Damas Bahianas* in the *Escola do Samba*, the frantic gestures of the *Pasistas*, and the deafening frenzy of the band.

Dancing is something about which one can rationalize only when one has finished it, not during it. Niemeyer's process of work and design is similar. It would seem, though, that he never quite reconsidered his works once they were finished. Therein lies both their freshness and their shortcomings. Although in his house at Canoas, near Rio de Janeiro (1953), he subtly searched to relate the form of the pond and the rock within the undulating slab of the roof, the forms do not really define a spatial existence; they merely pierce space without modifying its substance. This naturally has not always been the case: the concave-convex façade of the Hotel Copan (São Paulo, 1953–62) is not merely a gesticulation in a vacuum but the transformation of space into a *topos*. Niemeyer's imagination often leads him into structural acrobatics of dubious significance, which it would be incorrect to consider in the light of orthodox structural theories.

As his architecture evolved, another aspect became increasingly important. One could call it the dreamlike, almost science-fiction imagination which is more clearly defined in the models than in the actual works. The Petrópolis residential blocks of 1953 seem to have been imagined in a dream existence of their own. What would the model of the Museum of Modern Art for Caracas (*Fig. 8*) have yielded had it been built? It is difficult to see its almost incredible, fantastic image as anything more than a model. The more we think about it, the more it seems completely devoid of a true purposeful possibility. In Niemeyer's models there is always something very tempting, new, forcefully expressed, and buoyant. This brings us to the somewhat critical conclusion that his buildings are very often blown-up, full-scale models. With insufficient elaboration they lack that sense of completion which is the very essence of a true master-piece. However, on some occasions Niemeyer has produced very fine works such as the Hospital Sul America in Rio de Janeiro (1952–59), or the new Yacht Club in Pampulha (1961).

It would be very unjust to present the Brazilian movement from 1940 to 1956 as a one-man show. We should also mention the brothers Marcelo and Milton Roberto, architects of the A.B.I. Building (Rio de Janeiro, 1937) and the National Insurance Institute Building (Rio de Janeiro, 1942); Eduardo Affonso Reidy, architect of the Pedregulho housing development of 1950 near Rio de Janeiro (*Fig.*

7. *Oscar Niemeyer: Casa do Baile, Pampulha, Minas Geraes, Brazil, 1942.*

8. *Oscar Niemeyer: Museum of Modern Art, Caracas, Venezuela, 1955, model.*

9), and the Museum of Modern Art in Rio de Janeiro (1953); Osvaldo Arthur Bratke; Icaro de Castro Mello; Roberto Cerqueira César; Rino Levi; Henrique Mindlin; Paulo Antunes Ribeiro; and Sergio Bernardes.

Roberto Burle Marx's gardens, however, are Brazil's greatest contribution to the visual environment of our day. Since they are associated with much important contemporary Brazilian architecture, they are immediately related to the architectural experience and to urban design. Their plans give the feeling of loose curving contours interwoven with one another, yet the colored areas of the flower beds are always very distinct.

From *Hypnerotomachia Poliphili*[6] to Versailles, gardens depended on the classical theory of *decorum* and imposed a rational order on nature. Nature, although created by the Almighty, was considered imperfect; it was the artist's duty to bring order to it, or in other words to make it decorous. This theory reflected the conception of space as a system rather than a substratum. Burle Marx's gardens (*Fig. 10*) treat nature as a "given," yet not indifferent, existence that is more than a world of neutral objects. The gardens do not arise from the idea of *decorum*; their landscaping serves mainly

9. *Eduardo Affonso Reidy: Pedregulho housing development, Rio de Janeiro, Brazil, 1950.*

to enliven our experience of nature. It is an action by which something already there is made meaningful to us. But for this something to become meaningful it is necessary that the fundamental configuration of that which we perceive as being there should be held as a starting point. Since that which is "given" in nature is something very close to the first chance act in Hans Arp's paintings, it is not surprising to find an analogy between Arp's and Burle Marx's works.

Although most of Burle Marx's gardens are private ones, he has worked on a larger scale, as in the Parque del Este in Caracas (begun in 1957), and the Botanical Gardens of São Paulo (under execution). However, his main contribution to urban design is the Gloria-Flamingo Aterro in Rio de Janeiro (1963). These gardens, extending all along the new Beira Mar highway, were worked out according to two criteria. The central fringe gardens were designed with deep perspective, to be seen from speeding cars, while the area bordering the bay shores, more intimate in scale, took into account the pedestrians. It has always been rather difficult to understand why Burle Marx was excluded from Brasilia, as his contribution would have been decisive, but this is a subject we will develop later (pp. 35–41).

10. *Roberto Burle Marx: Gardens of Mrs. Odette Monteiro, Correas, Rio de Janeiro, Brazil, 1947.*

MEXICO

DURING the late twenties and the thirties, under the leadership of Villagrán García, Juan O'Gorman, Legorreta Yañez, and Enrique del Moral, Mexican architects came to regard ornament as a symptom of mental poverty. They built pure white boxes, whose inner walls José Clemente Orozco, Diego Rivera, and Alfaro David Siqueiros covered with huge frescoes that had the distinct accent of social protest. This movement ended in 1950.

It seems that at this date architects increasingly began to feel the inner artistical contradiction between the sense of the murals in their buildings and the buildings themselves. They strongly believed that architecture had a social propagandist role, and they seem to have concluded that their works were not really performing it. Perhaps this feeling became stronger as the growing conservatism of Mexican politics made it evident that the radical government leadership was ending. Perhaps also the International Style's loss of dominance was an influence; at any rate, from then on Mexican architects such as Yañez and O'Gorman were obsessed with finding a national architectural expression. Curiously enough, their aims became merged with a desire for an integration of the arts.

This desire has often been expressed by artists during this century, in very different forms. Piet Mondrian and the Constructivists proclaimed that painting and sculpture would merge into architecture. Le Corbusier was occupied with his concept of *synthèse des arts*, and the Bauhaus with a similar synthesis. Criticism had also developed a theory of the integration of arts, in its understanding of baroque art in relation to the concept of *Gesamtkunstwerk*, or total work of art.

Wilhelm Worringer thought that the integrative attitude characterized German art.[7] Mexicans came to the conclusion that it also typified pre-Columbian, pre-Cortesian, and colonial architecture. Thus, what seemed to them specifically Mexican did not quite correspond with the sense of rationality that had been expounded by Mexico's leading theorist of the thirties, Villagrán García. In short, this proposed artistic integration implied the use of large mosaic murals covering the building façades. These mosaic surfaces were worked out by Orozco, Rivera, and Siqueiros, and their later imitators. The result is a confused mixture of pre-Columbian and present-day motifs.

Juan O'Gorman's main library building in Mexico City's Ciudad

Universitaria is probably the most publicized example of all (*Fig. 11*). The contradiction between the pure stereometric forms of architecture and the rhythmic, chromatic violence of the candid anecdotes bursts wide open. It must be said in O'Gorman's defense that his original project, a sort of pyramid, differed completely from what was in fact built. His own home in San Angel, near Mexico City (*Fig. 12*), is a more accurate example of his endeavors. An uncontrolled fantastic imagination is at work there, and total rejection of reason unfolds in a succession of forms and spaces subdued to neither a constructive order nor a proportional principle. Set in a volcanic grotto, the work emerges out of nature as if the man-made and the natural were one.

The Mexican revival today has given way to curtain walls, but in a way it opened the way to Félix Candela's experience which we will discuss later.

11. *Juan O'Gorman, Gustavo Saavedra, and Juan Martinez de Velazco: Main library, Ciudad Universitaria, Mexico City, Mexico, 1953.*

12. *Juan O'Gorman: Architect's house, San Angel, Mexico, 1953, interior.*

ARGENTINA

UNLIKE his stay in Brazil, Le Corbusier's earlier visit to Buenos Aires in 1929 did not start a new movement. Since the Argentine establishment was absorbed in imitating the old Europe, only a restricted *inteligenzia* echoed his plea for a new urban culture. However, in June 1939 the Austral group published *Voluntad y Accion* (Will and Action), a manifesto reconsidering functional orthodoxy. It was said there that: "present day architecture finds itself not taking into account relative technical progress at a critical moment. The old spirit is all but gone. A new academy has emerged, a refuge of the mediocre. By misunderstanding the *machine à habiter* and by consciously ignoring individual psychology, functional architecture with all its aesthetic prejudices and infantile intransigencies, has arrived at intellectual and inhuman solutions."[8] At that time this was undoubtedly the most advanced program that any group in Latin America was proposing.

Antonio Bonet, a leading member, ignored International Style formulas in his Berlingieri House (*Fig. 13*) and even more clearly in his restaurant hostel, La Solana del Mar (*Fig. 14*). Although the former work may be related to Le Corbusier's Petite Maison de Weekend at Boulogne (1935) and to his Cherchell project in North Africa (1940), its articulation of space is quite different. The latter looks independent, and its relation toward landscape confirms this impression.[9]

However, Le Corbusier's influence was decisive in the early stages of the Austral group, as might be assessed in the apartment house by Jorge Ferrari Hardoy and Juan Kurchan in Buenos Aires (*Fig. 15*) which seems almost a materialization of Le Corbusier's ideal home symbolic structure, probably the only one ever to have come into existence.[10] This is not surprising if we remember that Bonet, Hardoy, and other members of the Austral group worked in Le Corbusier's office for almost two years just before World War II.[11] By 1947 they were evolving and reshaping Le Corbusier's masterplan for Buenos Aires. For a time it looked as if at least part of the huge scheme would be executed by 1948. However, the Argentine group was not so fortunate as Costa's Brazilian one, and all their major attempts, including the Belgrano housing development, were stopped by political interference immediately after construction had begun.

Eduardo Catalano's project for the Municipal Auditorium of Buenos Aires (1947), and Eduardo Sacriste's, Jorge Vivanco's, and

Horacio Comino's project for the Tucuman University campus (1948–49) showed that a section of the Austral group was evolving techniques and ideas quite independent of Le Corbusier's. Contrary to what we have seen in the case of Brazil and Mexico, the Austral members were not obsessed with national tradition, either because they felt Argentine architectural tradition was a poor source of inspiration, or because they believed that under present historical conditions, it was meaningless to look back to the past. They understood regionalism or national architecture in terms of social, economic, technical, and climatic problems, and they did not search in the direction of a colonial revival.

Amancio Williams was probably the most creative member of

13. *Antonio Bonet: Berlingieri house, Punta Ballena, Uruguay, 1946.*

14. *Antonio Bonet: La Solana del Mar, restaurant hostel, Punta Ballena, Uruguay, 1947.*

the generation; his Mar del Plata house is a most imaginative work of the period (*Figs. 16–17*). Here the idea of *promenade architecturale* takes a wholly original form. The house is raised over a structural arch. As one climbs into the living area, the curved, glazed staircase offers a simultaneous view of the landscape and the interior. The structure adequately fits the organization and the uses of space. Perfect detailing has always been one of Williams' obsessions, even before he knew Mies van der Rohe's work. His projects for an airport in the Rio de la Plata area (1945), for an auditorium (*Fig. 18*), and for a suspended office building (*Fig. 19*) are among the most audacious postwar architectural works.

Although a number of good buildings were executed during these years in Argentina, none of them found wide public response or government support as in Mexico and Brazil. However, a change in attitude had been brought about, and the younger architects who began their practice by the mid-fifties profited from the experience.

15. *Jorge Ferrari Hardoy and Juan Kurchan: Apartment house (Virrey del Pino 2664), Buenos Aires, Argentina, 1943.*

16. *Amancio Williams: Private house, Mar del Plata, Argentina, 1945.*

17. *Private house, Mar del Plata, elevation and plan.*

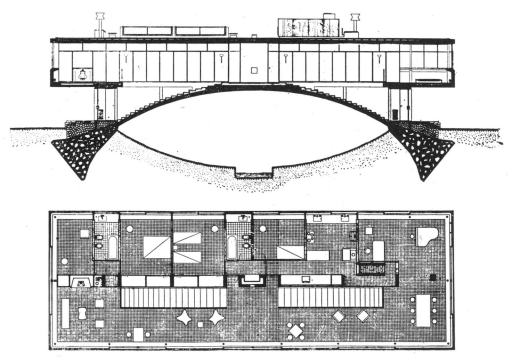

18. *Amancio Williams: Auditorium (Hall for Plastic Spectacle and Sound), 1943–53, model.*

19. *Amancio Williams: Suspended office building, 1948, project.*

URBAN UTOPIA AND REALITY

LATIN America has relentlessly pursued ideals of urban utopia, perhaps to a greater degree than the rest of the world. Nowhere else have modernistic urban theories, above all Le Corbusier's Ville Radieuse, controlled the minds of practicing architects and urban designers as much as in Latin America. A few early examples are the plans for Cidade dos Motores, Brazil, by José Luis Sert and Paul Lester Wiener (1942), for Medellin (1949-50), Tumaco (1948), and Bogotá (1951-53), all in Colombia and in association with the local planning staffs, and the Buenos Aires master-plan already mentioned. The construction of Brasilia marks the turning point in the Latin American experience and thus warrants special consideration.

These projects, like the Ville Radieuse, proceeded from several basic assumptions. First, it was assumed that a completely closed plan—a rigidly defined design that would not permit substantial changes—would solve once and for all the conflicts and contradictions of the industrial cities. Second, by implication, old city patterns were obsolete and therefore should be erased. The street, "a well trodden path of the eternal pedestrian, a relic of the centuries, a dislocated organ which can no longer function,"[12] should be eliminated. In its stead the *jardin anglais* on which tall blocks would rise should take its place. Automobile facilities should be given priority. Third, by further implication it would be necessary to subdivide the city into different areas according to function. Last but not least, it was maintained that communal ownership of the land was imperative, and that urban renewal under the control of a public agency would be both profitable and the only solution to the social, economic, and physical problems of the modern city.

The English "new town experience" has shown that only the last assumption is valid. It is rather difficult to believe that there may be a way to solve permanently the conflicts and contradictions which seem to be inherent in all urban cultures. It has been so in the past, it is so at present, and one does not very well see how it could be otherwise in the future. Conflicts and contradictions are dynamic elements essential to any kind of cultural evolution; this fact has to be accepted if one is determined to plan reality and not utopia. The assumption that the old parts of a city may be obliterated does not take into account that urban cultures are historical and therefore do not destroy what they feel is their heritage. There seems to be little hope that the *jardin anglais* will ever provide a real urban setting. The automotive utopia has already wrought havoc in many of the old cities, and the entire situation is being reconsidered throughout Latin America. Large urban deserts have appeared from indiscriminate use of automobile facilities, and the theory's enchantment is beginning to fade. Finally, that the city goes to pieces once a division of function has crystallized seems indisputable today.

Although it would seem that most of these assumptions are irrelevant when discussing the design of a new city, Brasilia was planned according to them and quite clearly exemplifies the shortcomings of such urban theories, in vogue until very recently. Erected in a record time of three years (1957–60), the city was planned in relation to Brazil's need to conquer physically, economically, and culturally its own continent-sized territory (*Figs. 20–23*).

The economic soundness of such an immense, short-term investment has been discussed at length. Some have objected that such a breathtaking effort almost crippled the country, and that a gradual process would have been more consistent with the plans for national development. Others have maintained that the political and economic instability of Latin American countries make long-term plans vulnerable and, furthermore, that capital always would tend to be reinvested in those already developed areas where initial costs were less. Therefore, clear-cut decisions which could be implemented immediately and would permit the settlement of the government during the presidency of Juscelino Kubitschek (1956–61), were imperative. Undoubtedly this policy in itself implied a closed plan for the new city, which is exactly what Lúcio Costa provided. As he states in his report, basically the plan arose "from the elementary gesture of one who marks or takes possession of a place." This gesture developed into two main axes, one urban and one traffic, out of which the city as a whole came into being (*Fig. 20*). Their intersection determined the center of the entire city and defined the central interchange of the road system. From the higher level of this central interchange is a breathtaking deep perspective of the civic center (*Fig. 21*), emphasizing that there, far in the distance, is the center of the new twentieth-century Brazil, the heart of its political, social, and economic power. The enchantment of the view lies in its utopic sense of a future as visualized in H. G. Wells' "Time to Come," and its sort of Flash Gordon sense of interplanetary adventure. The domed Senate and Assembly buildings far away look in the twilight like flying saucers almost floating on a platform where they are about to land or take off. Behind them the Secretariat building rises like a missile tower on the axis of the whole composition. But in spite of its modernistic aspect, the sweeping view relies more on a baroque principle of composition than on a contemporary principle of spatial organization. The Ministry buildings at either side of the axis further emphasize this effect.

To get an idea of the monumental scale employed, one should

realize that this eastern section of the civic axis is 2,000 meters long, almost the distance between the Place de la Concorde and the Etoile in Paris, and half the length of New York's Central Park. Consequently the civic center is very far from both the housing area and the business section. On the eastern end of the axis lies the Plaza of the Three Powers (*Fig. 22*). The surrounding buildings merely punctuate rather than enclose its space. They stand like sculptures, linked only by lines of force and tension like a neoplasticist composition. The distance between the Planalto Palace and the Supreme Court is almost a quarter of a mile; midway, the warriors by Bruno Giorgi try to make a brave stand under the strong tropical sun. To the east and beyond the Judiciary buildings, the eye travels straight

20. *Lúcio Costa and Oscar Niemeyer: Brasilia, Brazil, 1957–60, plan.*

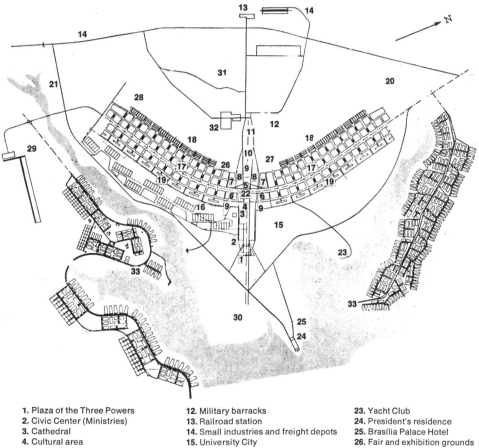

1. Plaza of the Three Powers	12. Military barracks	23. Yacht Club
2. Civic Center (Ministries)	13. Railroad station	24. President's residence
3. Cathedral	14. Small industries and freight depots	25. Brasilia Palace Hotel
4. Cultural area	15. University City	26. Fair and exhibition grounds
5. Entertainment center	16. Embassies and legations	27. Riding club
6. Banking and office area	17. Residential section	28. Cemetery
7. Trade center	18. Family dwellings	29. Airport
8. Hotels	19. Large living quarters	30. Golf club
9. Radio and television tower	20. Botanical Garden	31. Observatory
10. Sports center	21. Zoological Garden	32. Government printing office
11. Municipal plaza	22. Platform and traffic center	33. Private lots

to the line of hills around the city. There is a sort of dreamlike quality to the plaza. At first one is tempted to cross it, until he passes the warriors, when suddenly the dream becomes a nightmare and one feels he will never be able to make it.

It is fine to experience De Chirico's pictures, but actually to experience the sense of crawling like a pigmy on a pavement under the noon sun is something different. One suddenly realizes that the plaza has never been used by anybody except oneself; or perhaps it was fully occupied by an enthusiastic crowd only on the day of the city's dedication. The President came to the balcony of the Planalto Palace and delivered his historic message "Urbi et Orbi," but after that nothing ever really happened at the plaza. The center

21. *Brasilia, civic axis looking toward civic center.*

22. *Brasilia, Plaza of the Three Powers. Left, Museum. Right, Planalto Palace and "The Warriors" by Bruno Giorgi.*

of power is far too removed from the inhabitants to enable them to participate, even though they are mostly government officials.

The Ministerial mall looks rather suspiciously perfect: all the buildings are of equal orientation and identical form. It is not clear why sun protection has been eliminated. In any case, there seems to be sufficient space for inevitable expansions and modifications, without jeopardizing the layout. The new building of the Foreign Affairs Ministry leads one to suppose that the repetitive character of the Ministerial mall in time will be somewhat transformed. The monumental axis is further complemented by the cathedral, the National Theater, and other cultural buildings. To the north and south of the cultural section are two banking and office areas.

The central traffic interchange divides the monumental axis in two equal parts: the eastern one already described, and the western one which has as a focus point the television and radio tower and ends with the municipal plaza. Symmetrically located along the sides are the entertainment center, the hotel area, and the main business section of the city. In short, Brasilia's downtown area is in the proximity of the central traffic interchange, where the bus terminal is situated. This decision does not seem very wise, considering the atmosphere generally surrounding bus terminals. Furthermore, only time will tell the wisdom of concentrating all the traffic pressure in one point.

The central traffic interchange has three levels. The lower is underground and will be used by through traffic moving along the north-south axis; the upper will be used by traffic going into the entertainment and business areas; and the middle will connect the north-south axis traffic with the east-west. The north-south, or residential axis, does not run in a straight line but curves in the form of a bow. It links the residential areas to the downtown and civic areas and joins the national road system at both the north and south ends. It also connects the city to the airport.

The central artery of fourteen lanes, fed by access highways winding among the *supercuadras* (residential units), seems more than sufficient to bear future traffic loads. A secondary traffic system has been provided for symmetrically at both sides of the north-south axis. Within the area formed by these avenues and cross streets rise the *supercuadras* (*Fig. 23*). Each *supercuadra* is a lot 240 meters square on which are 8 to 11 six-story apartment blocks. A neighborhood unit consists of four *supercuadras* and groups of shops, a supermarket, chapel, movie theater, nursery and primary school, social-recreational club, and clinic. However, one feels that the mechanical inclusion of these elements is not enough to create a neighborhood urban reality. Through traffic is absent in the *supercuadras*, and automobiles seem admitted only on sufferance. Coaches and mini-buses provided by the various government departments to take their employees to work seem to solve the traffic problem, but will continue to do so just as long as only public servants inhabit the *supercuadras*, and as long as they do not own and drive many automobiles. Although even with an increase in cars there would be enough parking space for everyone in the *supercuadras*, and most of the area would still be free for social use, it does not seem that the access road system would be able to bear the corresponding traffic load.

The buildings in each *supercuadra* are distributed according to a standard layout. Although they may look rather boring and repetitious on paper, the urban spaces are in fact more varied than one would assume. The same cannot be said about the apartment blocks themselves. The inhabitants' resentment of the monotonous design of the façade is clear from their use of the framed concrete façade elements in order to gain some kind of identity. They have transformed the concrete frames into receptacles for bicycles, kitchen pots, or whatever. The apartment buildings are not really able to create a significant order in which individual initiative can assert itself. Another main drawback of this schematic approach is the orientation of identical buildings in several directions with almost no concern whatever for the sun. It is unfortunate that Oscar Niemeyer, already over-burdened with designing all the public buildings, did not accept the collaboration of other architects who perhaps would have had more time to study thoroughly the design of the residential areas.

23. *Brasilia,* supercuadra *(residential unit).*

This leads us back to the important matter of the shortcomings of instant planning and dictatorial leadership. A city must be not a one-man show, but the result of the contributions of several architects and of the general public; this coordination seems to have been lacking in Brasilia. Totalitarian closed planning does not really work either on the scale of the apartment buildings and the neighborhood units, or on the vaster scale of the city as a whole. Even before Costa's original layout was put into practice it had to undergo some important changes. The two peninsulas between the arms of the lake had come to be thought appropriate for suburban housing, necessitating an extension of the previously closed plan. Although, for the time being this extension might not create an urban sprawl—which Brasilia fortunately still lacks—once the principle is accepted, one does not see very well how future pressures will not open the doors to additional expansions.

This brings us to conclude that urban planning can only be, to use a Joycean expression, a "work in progress," which means virtually organizing the process of growth and change according to a project subjected to patterns, not to an a priori definite total form. "The failure of a *project* opens the doors to the disorder of *destiny*."[13]

The Cidade Livre or Free Town some ten miles from the center of Brasilia is a proof of this conclusion. Although it began as temporary housing for the laborers, it is now there to stay. Thus, closed city planning has been caught in the shanty-town dilemma. As elsewhere, an effort was made to dislodge the inhabitants when their temporary permits expired, and as elsewhere, it failed. A spontaneous wild west, shanty-town life has arisen, which contrasts with the formality of the city itself, and which has become too valuable to be destroyed. This brings us to one of the main problems confronting architects all over Latin America today.

Everywhere shanty towns have grown up accompanying the expansion of cities and industry. Although at first they were looked upon as only a problem of housing, they are far more complicated. Housing involves transportation facilities, schools, cultural centers, business facilities, and so forth. Until very recently it has been assumed that the problem of shanty town belts could be solved by resettling the population and by investing large amounts of capital in housing developments, thus both obtaining social stability and scoring a political success for the governing party.

Perhaps the most ambitious efforts in this direction were the 23 de Enero, El Paraiso, and Cerro Piloto highrise housing developments in Caracas, built in several stages between 1955 and 1957 by the Workers Bank of Caracas (*Figs. 24–26*). Carlos Raúl Villanueva headed the design team and developed the basic program in association with Guido Bermudez, Carlos Brando, Juan Centella, José Mijares, and Carlos Celis Cepero. Organizing such a monumental relocation of people who knew nothing of urban life, preparing the

24. *Carlos Raúl Villanueva and others: 23 de Enero housing development, Caracas, Venezuela, 1955–57, aerial view.*

25. *23 de Enero housing development, superblocks.*

financial plans, and building the huge blocks, all were in themselves admirable.[14] But as in so many of the Latin American attempts based on developed countries' prototypes, the housing units met with flat resistance by the people. This resulted not only from the dictatorial methods often employed in moving the shanty town inhabitants from their quarters to the new palatial surroundings, but mainly from the basic conflict between the cultural patterns of the immigrant rural population and those forced onto it. The toilet seat used as a frame for grandmother's photo portrait is only one symbol of the difficulties to be surmounted. Undoubtedly more important is the misuse of connecting corridors and elevators by people who are in the habit of chatting with their neighbors in their doorways, or the failure to maintain the *jardin anglais*, which has turned into wasteland. The approach we have been discussing is no longer tenable.

Naturally the solution is not simple, and architects vacillate between different approaches. Proposals range from insisting on authoritarian attitudes to building transitional housing that would help assimilate the immigrants into the existing urban patterns of behavior. The latter attitude conceals a desire to impose on others what those in command feel is a legitimate way of life, while ignoring what the squatters themselves can bring of cultural value.

In Lima, a government agency, the Junta Nacional de la Vivienda de Peru, is developing a third possibility and new direction, a barriada which takes into account not only the above considerations and

26. *Carlos Raúl Villanueva and others: Cerro Piloto housing development, Caracas, Venezuela, 1955–57, superblocks.*

facts of urban life, but also the Latin American economy's incapacity to deal with the problem on a short-term basis. Statistically, it is quite clear that even a country with a high per capita income, such as Argentina, would take at least fifty-two years to solve its housing problem, and then only if the rate of dwellings constructed yearly reached the level of eight per thousand inhabitants, which would require the housing investment rate to double. Nations with a greater housing deficiency would have to increase this investment even more. When one considers housing investment policies in relation to the overall investment problems of Latin American countries, which direly need to obtain a higher rate of capital investment in other areas of their economy, one soon realizes that housing investment can increase only at the expense of those areas that would, in the long run, bring about an expansion of the economy. This dilemma is becoming recognized throughout the continent, as is the fact that its solution will require a complete reversal of present policies. Thus the Lima barriada experience becomes a new option, out of which a new direction in architecture and city planning will evolve.

The Junta Nacional de la Vivienda is basing its work not on utopian theories but on the following given facts by which the barriada came into existence: that the illegal occupation of vacant or private land cannot be stopped; that a social organization exists within the barriada community which is not only concerned with internal order but which previously made possible the illegal settlement; that, even if government aid is not forthcoming, the majority of the urban working class will take matters into its own hands and solve at least part of its housing and community development problems on its own initiative and outside the established order; that this marginal communal organization has enough energy and its members enough ability, perseverance, and power of organization, as well as slowly accumulated savings, to make an important contribution; and that the rural traditions and skills of city immigrants cannot, unaided, respond quickly or adequately to the violent changes demanded by urban conditions. However, if government assistance is provided in the way of land acquisition, services, infra-structures, and technology, a suitable policy which may avoid great and permanent losses might be implemented.

Obviously self-help introduces a number of problems for the planner and architect willing to contribute their effort. The barriada is the paradigm of work in progress, as most owners will build their houses in stages from a minimal nucleus. While adapting to changing needs, desires, and opportunities, the owners will insist on their own values; a mutual respect of designer and owner-builder must mature so that together they can seek solutions.

The differentiation among land, buildings, and public utilities is even more important than it at first appears, as the critic John Turner clearly understood. "The provision of each of these elements

27. *Carlos Bresciani, Hector Valdés, Fernando Castillo, and Carlos G. Huidobro: Portales neighborhood unit, Quinta Normal, Santiago, Chile, 1959–61, apartment buildings and row houses.*

28. *Portales neighborhood unit, pedestrian street and apartment buildings.*

requires a different procedure and therefore different skills, and type of organization, and this not only gives full scope to the contribution of the future owners, but also gives the housing agencies involved much more administrative freedom, by programming the provision of each element separately, instead of treating them as a package deal." Last but not least the overall concern of the sponsoring agency should be to work with, not for, the groups and families taking part.[15]

However, the middle income bracket, with its urban tradition and higher standard of living, demands other solutions. Among a number of successful developments perhaps the Portales neighborhood unit, at Quinta Normal (state technical university), Santiago, by Carlos Bresciani, Hector Valdés, Fernando Castillo, and Carlos G. Huibobro should receive special consideration (*Figs. 27–31*). The unit is built in a section of the old agricultural park, a popular recreation center which since the beginning of the century has become engulfed by the growth of Santiago. The construction was financed by a state agency, the Corporación de la Vivienda (C.O.R.V.I.), which provided the middle- and lower-income brackets with housing strictly controlled as to acceptable costs and reasonably practical solutions. The inhabitants were carefully screened for occupation, income, and so forth. The space allotted per bed was established at a maximum of 17.5 square meters including the area occupied by the structure and circulation. The maximum area per unit could not exceed 140 square meters; until 1959 the use of elevators was prohibited, which limited the height of the buildings. The designers, accepting these limitations, refusing to build on large tree-covered areas of the lot, and taking advantage of a two-degree decline in the ground toward the west, decided on a solution which was at that time being explored by Jack Lynn and his associate in Park Hill, Sheffield, England. Open bridges and pedestrian ramps link the apartment blocks with the business center. Stairwells in the centers of the blocks connect the different levels of the buildings themselves. The regulation limiting the height of buildings to walk-up access (five stories) was observed, while two more stories were gained below the access level. A high level pedestrian street connects all the buildings; in an emergency it can be used by cars and is therefore linked to vehicular ramps located in strategic positions. It also stretches above single-story row houses at treetop level. Thus a social space is provided for the communal interaction which, in Latin American society, usually takes place on the sidewalk in front of the house entrance doors. This plan thus avoids some of the problems that result from heavy traffic in the streets.

Typical five-story walk-up blocks with a distant view of the center of Santiago have different sorts of apartment units and maisonettes on top floors. The single-story houses are placed in the courts between the five-story terraces. The repetitious structures

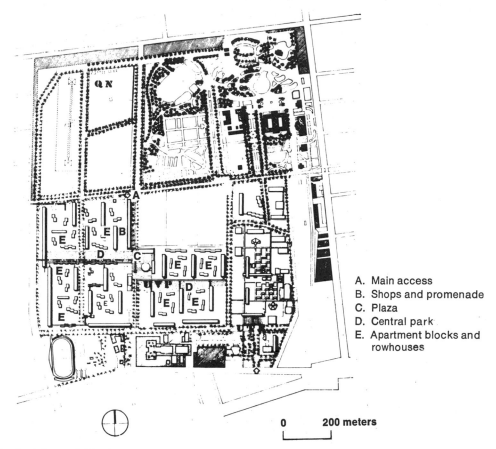

A. Main access
B. Shops and promenade
C. Plaza
D. Central park
E. Apartment blocks and
   rowhouses

0   200 meters

29. *Portales neighborhood unit, plan. Right, Quinta Normal.*

30. *Portales neighborhood unit, detail.*

are all of reinforced concrete. Finish is minimal throughout, the concrete generally being left off the shuttering. As is common in Latin America, the standard of finish in the concrete work is excellent. At the end of the five-story blocks are free-standing access stairs, worked out in a rather sculptural shape. The apartments are screened from the sun by plastic blinds in three standard colors: gray, bright blue, and yellow.

The neighborhood unit is composed of two areas, east and west, between which is the principal pedestrian and automobile access to the neighborhood. This access, along which the business area is located, ends up in a plaza which is surrounded by the market, a church, a movie theater, and so on, and which is the social sector of the neighborhood unit. The high pedestrian street system converges toward this plaza. As we have seen, vehicular traffic surrounds the neighborhood and invades it in only two points. The only central traffic way crosses from north to south and is sunken. A bridge connecting the east and west has been provided for pedestrians.

31. *Portales neighborhood unit, access stairs at end of apartment blocks.*

TOWNSCAPE ARCHITECTURE

MODERN architecture was born rejecting the past. The fathers had to be killed to let their sons grow. While the new architecture underwent its long and strained adolescent crisis, no other approach was really possible, although today its infantility is readily apparent. Nineteenth-century values and works were regarded as empty and treated with scorn.

In its turn, the new generation no longer regards attitudes of the Bauhaus or Adolf Loos as indisputable, and though it respects the earlier vocabulary it no longer feels attuned to it. This is clear from the headquarters of the Bank of London and South America, in Buenos Aires, by Clorindo Testa in association with Santiago Sanchez Elía, Federico Peralta Ramos, and Alfredo Agostini (S.E.P.R.A.) (*Figs. 32–37*). Here the architects tried to establish a continuity of scale and mass which would blend with the surrounding buildings, contrary to what would have been the polemical attitude of prewar architecture.

Le Corbusier never accepted the street; Testa and his associates intended to preserve it as a daily urban experience. A street is, after all, a longitudinal space created by buildings. One destroys it as soon as one begins to articulate its longitudinal space with transversal open plazas. Now, a street in a city must have an identity of its own, or it is devoid of all meaning. This identity grows from the contribution of successive generations. To preserve a street as a daily urban experience, a dialogue must take place: if the society in which one builds has or needs streets, and one plans to build on a street, he cannot ignore what lies across from his building, for inevitably it will interfere.

The architects of the Bank of London based their project on this thesis. Given were two narrow streets used mainly by pedestrians (across one was the imposing mass of the Banco Nación, on the other, early twentieth-century Beaux-Arts buildings) and providing no distant, all-embracing perspective of the bank. As another given, the bank had stressed its need for a unified inner space, especially in the banking area. From these two demands rose both the structural scheme and the resulting façade treatment, which implied in themselves an inner spatial organization and a relationship between inner and outer space (*Figs. 32–33*).

The structural, upright, fanlike piers contribute both to establish the desired scale relationship and to limit solidly the street space,

32. *Clorindo Testa, Santiago Sanchez Elía, Federico Peralta Ramos, and Alfredo Agostini (S.E.P.R.A.): Bank of London and South America, headquarters, Buenos Aires, Argentina, 1960–66, entrance.*

33. *Bank of London and South America, headquarters, façade.*

while enabling the elimination of all structural members in the inner grand banking hall. The piers are complemented by planes (some of which are recessed) with huge oblong, curved perforations, which provide a visually strong, varied experience. Thus the pedestrian, lacking a complete view, obtains knowledge of the work as he progresses into it. Parts which are consistent with one another and which do not negate the structural value enable him to understand a reality that he sees first as accidental but finally as ordered. From the outside the façade seems closed, so that he can only peep in here and there. From the inside, though, he suddenly realizes that the inner unified space is confined only by the façade of the building across the street. The huge, empty space of the bank's main entrance on the corner articulates the encounter of the two façades. This transitional space both acknowledges the interior space and serves as a covered plaza where the long street chats take place.

From the plaza the pedestrian continues into one of the most imaginative spaces of postwar architecture, one of almost Piranesian complexity (*Figs. 35–37*). It is a five-story unified space in which the upper three hanging levels seem to float, while the lower two are supported by cantilevered structures. Horizontal planes, linked with bridges, pierce space and have no contact at all either with the glass screen that slides behind the façade structure or with the dividing walls. The central well-like space is dominated by two vigorous towers whose pivotal effect suggests a dynamic opposition

34. *Bank of London and South America, headquarters, entrance hall.*

of mass and space. Every detail of the perfect concrete finish was conceived in such a way that no retouching was necessary in order to link the concrete surface with other finishings. Vertical air-conditioning pipes, clearly visible, are painted with bright colors. The horizontal ducts have been integrated into the railings which thus acquire a double function. Every part is a visual synthesis in itself, and contributes to building up the huge *inscape.*

One senses in the interior, as in the exterior, that the entire building is the result of an effort to find more than a point, a line, or a method common to both fantasy and reason. There is no feeling of coinage, or of the *gravitas* of traditional pseudo-Roman banking architecture, but rather an atmosphere of computer efficiency and security. It is not a world of dreams, because everything clearly shows why it has been put there.

Criticism of the Bank of London building always brings to the fore the problem of the meaning of technology in underdeveloped countries. This immediately brings a wide range of topics into our discussion.

35. *Bank of London and South America, headquarters, banking hall.*

36. *Bank of London and South America, headquarters, banking hall.*

37. *Bank of London and South America, headquarters, banking hall.*

TECHNOLOGY AND
ARCHITECTURE

IN Mexico, Augusto Alvarez and Enrique de la Mora favor curtain walls because they feel they are the only antidote for the anachronistic attitude of the pre-Columbian revival. Unfortunately, this trend often results in passive imitations of work north of Rio Grande. Enrique de la Mora's building for the Compañía de Seguros Monterrey, Mexico City, is clearly more experimental (*Fig. 38*). Two hollow concrete shafts reach from the ground to the seventh floor, where they support two enormous longitudinal concrete beams. These in turn support transverse armatures on which the building is "hung." Structurally this is closely related to the Bank of London and to Amancio Williams' suspended office buildings.

On the other hand, Eladio Dieste of Uruguay, convinced that "we won't have heavy industry in the immediate future," and grieving for a "human ingenuity which might get lost as an infinitely precious gem falling from our hands into the bottom of the ocean," intends to make the very best use of the bricklayers' craftmanship. "The worker who inhabits the most insignificant little town, and carries bricks in his blood" is to Dieste "the most worthy capital."[16] Under the circumstances, aping the technology of highly developed countries makes no sense at all. This does not mean a renunciation of rationalism, nor does it imply a "sentimental attitude opposed to progress." Dieste's technological outlook rests less on a complicated paraphernalia than on a clear pursuit of scientific fundamentals of the behavior of materials.

"Often," he says, "when I talk to students and tell them that our attitude towards concrete structures is a nineteenth-century one, and that it is not adjusting itself to the possibilities of reinforced concrete, I read in their eyes the obvious question—why not? The honest answer is because we do not yet know how to change. The structures on which I have been working resist analysis. Or, if it can be used, it requires such a heavy mathematical instrumentation of unusual complexity that it cannot be separated easily into rapid calculation elements. . . . Qualitative research demands a lot of patience, and one has to learn to free one's mind of previous schemes, to refine the research with a vigilant spirit, and last but not least, to have courage and audacity."[17]

The use of brick goes back to the dawn of human civilization. Until recently it has been used basically as a material suitable for admitting compression stresses. Flexion, which implied traction in certain parts of a building's sections, was avoided. In the case of vaults and domes, very heavy sections were introduced to insure that the structure's own weight would counter all accidental loads. This practice led to huge loads and consequently strong supporting sections. The inclusion of steel grids between bricks enabled them to accept traction stresses, and opened up a new horizon of possibilities. This is the area which Dieste has explored.

His works are more than engineering puzzles, however. Although they look complicated, they are essentially very simple. The fact that Dieste, like Félix Candela, fully controls the execution insures perfect finishing. But the value of his work is based mainly on a fantastic imagination: every part of wall or roofing attracts our attention because any and all of them are intimately united to the total form. The church of Atlántida (*Figs. 39–43*) and the T. E. M. sheds (*Fig. 44*) are among his most successful works.

38. *Enrique de la Mora and Fernando Gonzalez Pozo: Compañía de Seguros Monterrey building, Mexico City, Mexico, 1960.*

39. *Eladio Dieste: Church, Atlántida, Uruguay, 1958, detail of exterior.*

40. *Church, Atlántida, detail of exterior.*

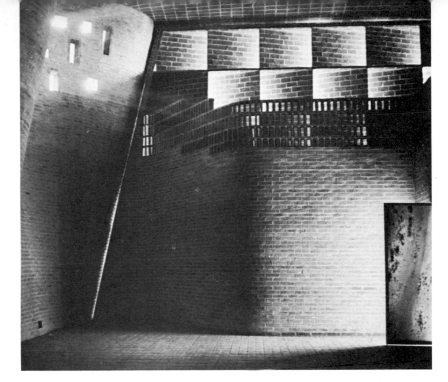

41. *Church, Atlántida, detail of interior.*

42. *Church, Atlántida, belltower staircase.*

43. *Church, Atlántida, detail of vaults.*

44. *Eladio Dieste: Talleres Electricos Montevideo (T.E.M.) shed, Montevideo, Uruguay, 1960,
detail of interior.*

In this connection we must mention the work of Félix Candela, which has attracted universal interest and admiration. Candela's approach, based on a rejection of positivism, develops from a careful consideration of the behavior of materials to a very simple process of execution. The classical hypothesis of the isotropic character of materials, and of the proportional relation between stresses and deformations is outdated with respect to the use of concrete.

Although Candela never comments on the visual significance of his works, it is not lacking, as is so insistently proposed at present. Though many architects may be officially credited as the creators of different works, we have little difficulty in recognizing the unmistakable hand of Félix Candela, for his designs have a sense of proportion and definition of profiles that can only be his. Most of his works have been warehouses, markets, and industrial buildings (*Figs. 45–46*), but some churches have also come from his drawing board, particularly in association with Enrique de la Mora (*Figs. 47–50*).

45. *Félix Candela: Bacardi bottling plant, Cuatitlán, Mexico, 1963.*

46. *Bacardi bottling plant, interior.*

47. *Félix Candela and Enrique de la Mora: Iglesia de Nuestra Señora de la Soledad, Coyoacán, Mexico, 1956, side view.*

48. *Iglesia de Nuestra Señora de la Soledad, interior.*

49. *Félix Candela and Enrique de la Mora: Iglesia San Vicente de Paul, Mexico City, Mexico, 1959–60, interior.*

50. *Félix Candela: Iglesia de la Medalla Milagrosa, Mexico City, Mexico, 1954, interior.*

In his works, structural form conceived as an integrated whole emerges as an expression of the plastic qualities of reinforced concrete, as a vital organism which unfolds as a continuous structure, and not as an inert form apt to be analyzed by section (*Fig. 51*). However, there is none of the willful originality often seen in other recent structuralist attempts.

Yet another point of view regarding technology—the ideological approach—seems to be implied in Ricardo Porro's and Vittorio Garatti's art schools in Havana (*Figs. 52–59*), as well as Claudio Caveri and Eduardo Ellis' Iglesia Nuestra Señora de Fátima at Martinez, Argentina (although here the intention may be almost opposite to that in the Cuban examples) (*Figs. 60–61*). Caveri and Ellis have built a *béton brut* and whitewashed brick structure in an agonized search for a Christian revival in the context of national expression. However, this obviously has little or nothing to do with the vaginal suggestions in Porro's vaulted passages or with his breastlike domes, and still less with exulting sense of revolutionary ardor implied in the broken order of his layouts (*Figs. 52–55*). Then shortage of materials affected the basic attitude of both Porro and Garatti, but it would appear that an excitement arising from the revolutionary winds sweeping Cuba at the time was the more profound influence.

Although Garatti's schools of music and ballet do not explicitly resort to the Afro-Cuban experience or to sexual imagery, they very much assert a spirit of free invention that seems also to have been Porro's main concern. From the plan, the serpentine form of the Music School seems to unfold continuously, but in reality this is not the case. Again, as in Porro's School of Plastic Arts, the whole has been fragmented, and the cumulative quality of the parts has not been subsumed. As in Christo's "packages" or Arman's "accumulations" the individual forms subsist and make sense only through their "random" accumulation.

Garatti's domes and vaults at the Ballet School (*Figs. 56–58*) have been thoroughly studied for their static behavior and their construction, but these aspects do not seem to be the decisive consideration. The school at first appears to be the result of a sweeping impulse, but again no form is completed, no formal succession is accepted, no order seems pre-established, and no final balance seems to have been desired. In short, it appears to express clearly revolutionary Cuba's mood in the early sixties.

The first-hour Cuban saturnalia, represented by these art schools and by the huge East Havana housing complex built by a team from the Ministry of Construction, has come to an end. As Fidel Castro has warned, such high-standard accommodations are more than the country can afford. (This does not mean, however, that controls have been imposed on the architects' creativity. J. M. Richards has drawn attention to the remarkable freedom from prejudice, even by western standards, that he met in Cuba.[18])

51. *Félix Candela: "Umbrellas," Mexico.*

52. *Ricardo Porro: Plastic Arts School, Havana, Cuba, 1962–65, aerial view.*

53. *Plastic Arts School, patio.*

54. *Plastic Arts School, vaults.*

55. *Ricardo Porro: Modern Dance School, Havana, Cuba, 1963–65, aerial view.*

56. *Vittorio Garatti: Ballet School, Havana, Cuba, 1963–64, aerial view.*

57. *Ballet School, detail of exterior.*

58. *Ballet School.*

An indication that neoexpressionism is fading out appears not only in the more recent work of Garatti himself, but also in Havana's J. A. Echeverría University campus, by a team headed by José Fernandez (*Fig. 62*), and in such housing developments as Manicaragua, at Las Villas, by Fernando Salinas (*Fig. 63*).

The "urban" solution for the Manicaragua housing complex was imposed by the need to find housing situated in a natural environment for the technicians of a factory. Its urbanistic composition revolves freely and fluidly around the "axial" street, which is the means of social circulation and interaction. The original construction system is one of Cuba's first experimental steps in prefabrication. All the semi-heavy concrete sections were created from only one formal plan and three basic moulds. The recurring theme of concave shapes establishes a linguistic coherence. The limited finish of the structure and the oversimplified treatment of the functional accessories are proof that a final study of this system is yet to be made.

On the outskirts of Santiago de Cuba, the José Martí district, although of a very poor urban design indeed, marks the first Cuban effort to use a large panel prefab system. Most of the new housing and planning is presently concentrated in the rural areas and tends to keep the population there, in cooperation with the economic master-plan which sees increased agricultural output as a prerequisite for future intensive industrial investment. The rural communities thus respresent the first stages of a new direction.

59. *Vittorio Garatti: Music School, Havana, Cuba, 1963–65, façade.*

60. *Claudio Caveri and Eduardo Ellis: Iglesia Nuestra Señora de Fátima, Martinez, province of Buenos Aires, Argentina, 1957, interior.*

61. *Iglesia Nuestra Señora de Fátima.*

62. *José Fernandez and others: J. A. Echeverria University campus, Havana, Cuba, 1964–65, Technological Institute building.*

63. *Fernando Salinas: Manicaragua housing development, Las Villas, Cuba, 1964.*

Vittorio Garatti emerges as the most promising architect in Cuba today. His Technological Soil and Fertilizing Institute at Güines (*Figs. 64–65*) shows a change from his earlier works, in both layout and detailing. It is, however, in his Cuban pavilion at Expo '67 (*Figs. 66–68*) that a really new attitude becomes evident. It does not return to the "less is more" theory which, in fact, Garatti considers as "less is a bore." It is geometrical in terms of a pop art three-dimensional experience. The large interior display space, reached by exterior stairs, is squarely presented; for the rest, a push-and-pull geometry accommodates ventilating machinery, film projection apparatus, and several outdoor screens. The interior has been worked out in relation to direct political and social propaganda which, after all, is the scope of any such pavilion. Its use of photo montages and film projection shows that Garatti is fully aware of trends and aspirations in "media-massaged" societies.

64. *Vittorio Garatti: Technological Soil and Fertilizing Institute, Güines, Cuba, 1964, aerial view.*

65. *Technological Soil and Fertilizing Institute.*

66. *Vittorio Garatti, Sergio Baroni, and M. Da Costa: Cuban pavilion, Expo '67, Montreal, Quebec, 1967.*

67. *Cuban pavilion.*

68. *Cuban pavilion.*

CARLOS RAÚL VILLANUEVA

THE preceding chapter leads us to another Expo '67 example, the Venezuelan pavilion by Carlos Raúl Villanueva (*Figs. 69–70*). That a minimal sculpture represented Venezuela may have surprised many critics, but not the ones who know of Villanueva's work. A trio of solid aluminium cubes, brightly painted and linked by a glass entrance, sits firmly on a podium. The primary geometry and the bold typography create a lack of scale which obviously sets the exhibit apart from the surrounding fair atmosphere and draws attention to the stunning compositional effects of the shining cubes reflecting on each other.

This does not seem to be the work of a sixty-eight-year-old man who in 1941 was building El Silencio apartment blocks and plaza (*Fig. 71*). However, along with the project for the Museo de Bellas Artes in Caracas (*Fig. 72*), it is proof of the vitality of one of Latin America's most important architects. In order to understand Villanueva's present endeavors we should consider some of his earlier works, of which the Ciudad Universitaria of Caracas is one of the most influential (*Figs. 73–74*). Its Aula Magna or great hall (*Figs. 75–80*) and School of Architecture (*Figs. 81–83*) deserve special mention. In our opinion, with the Aula Magna's interior space Villanueva's artistic synthesis reached its summit, creating true values of space and completely merging the architectural work with that of the sculptor, Alexander Calder. The spectator experiences a very important element of surprise as he is led from the exterior through the expanded space of the covered plaza that converges progressively toward the circular foyer with its ramps, until he is abruptly confronted with the undefined space of the great hall. But once there, the surprise over, he continues to be irresistibly attracted by space whose precise limits he cannot begin to define. Although, the pit descending toward the stage constitutes a resting point for the eye, the play of lights and floating, concave planes of Calder, and Villanueva's acoustical sails attract his attention.

The light, which dynamically transforms and reconstructs the optical dimensions of the hall, brings out a few planes from the veiled depths and catches others while quickly flashing across the space. One's attention pivots from one center to another, resting on forms that seem to hide in a transparent colored shadow, or chasing the series of rectangular and oblique lights on the walls, which flee on encountering the luminous circles reflected on the ceiling. This

69. *Carlos Raúl Villanueva: Venezuelan pavilion, Expo '67, Montreal, Quebec, 1967.*

70. *Venezuelan pavilion.*

71. *Carlos Raúl Villanueva: El Silencio, Caracas, Venezuela, 1941, plaza.*

72. *Carlos Raúl Villanueva: Museo de Bellas Artes, Caracas, Venezuela, 1968, model.*

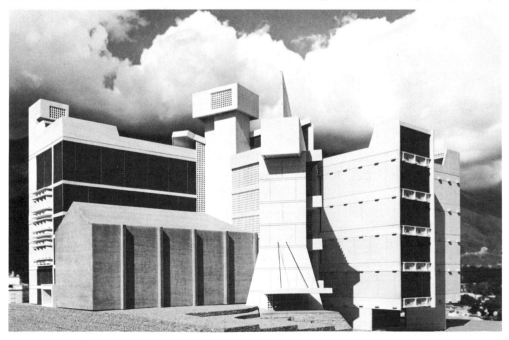

73. *Carlos Raúl Villanueva: Ciudad Universitaria, Caracas, Venezuela, 1952, aerial view.*

74. *Ciudad Universitaria, covered plaza.*

dynamic game, which includes the highest balcony, which seems to be projected over the whole scene, finally resolves itself on reaching the stage, where the practical significance of all this lyrical development becomes apparent. Advised by the acoustical engineer, Robert B. Newman, the architect has contrived to create not only an acoustically perfect hall but also an outstanding poetic reality. The exterior of the Aula Magna therefore acquires full importance as a structure which houses, with dry somber grandiosity, the visual spectacle that unfolds in its interior. The covered plaza, that vast shady area that shelters the visitor from the tropical sun, is an ideal resting place. Here and there the light intensely penetrates it, illuminating the curved or planar murals by Fernand Léger, Victor Vasarely, Mateo Manaure, and Navarro, or resting on the sculptures of Hans Arp and Henri Laurens, or revealing some tropical flora. It is true that an adequate linguistic synthesis was not always maintained, perhaps because it was not possible to keep in direct contact with the artists beyond supplying them with a model of the plaza.

The School of Architecture, situated in the angle of the university city, also merits detailed analysis. It is a block inserted in a group of workshops for visual study, composition, and construction. Displayed freely behind them and on the same level are an auditorium, a large exhibition hall, and a museum. Apparently with this

75. *Ciudad Universitaria, Aula Magna, foyer.*

76. *Ciudad Universitaria, Aula Magna, auditorium.*

77. *Ciudad Universitaria, Aula Magna, auditorium.*

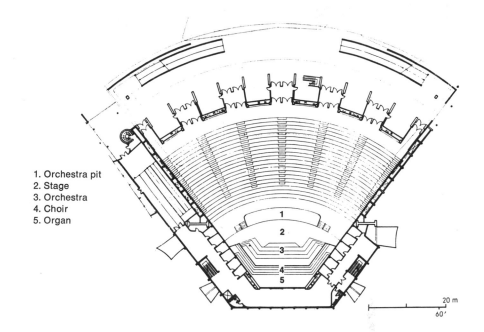

1. Orchestra pit
2. Stage
3. Orchestra
4. Choir
5. Organ

20 m

60'

78. *Ciudad Universitaria, Aula Magna, plan.*

79. *Ciudad Universitaria, Aula Magna, longitudinal and transverse sections.*

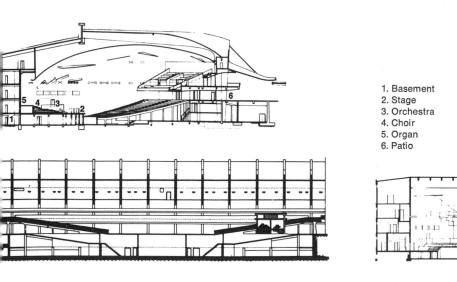

1. Basement
2. Stage
3. Orchestra
4. Choir
5. Organ
6. Patio

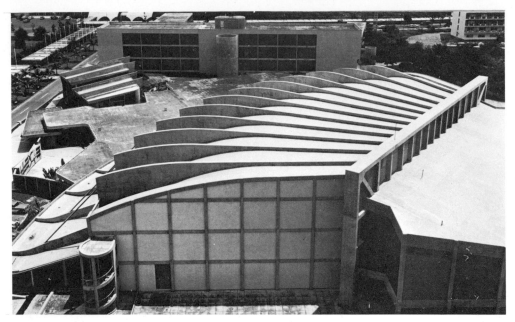

80. *Ciudad Universitaria, Aula Magna, detail of exterior.*

81. *Ciudad Universitaria, School of Architecture, façade.*

group Villanueva decided to favor the synthesis of art (a theme that we have seen is one of his principle preoccupations) and not to allow the crystallization of didactic functions, by shaping an elastic subdividable or open space dependent on changing requirements. In this latter sense, if the modular solutions adopted in the building's higher floors are foreseeable, the solution reached in the lower parts, especially in the workshops, is far from the beaten track, and is an invitation to the imaginative experience of space, ever more commendable in a building of this nature.

82. *Ciudad Universitaria, School of Architecture, detail of façade.*

Yet it is perhaps on the exterior that Villanueva's concern for developing a subtle visual experience achieves its maximum expression. The elevator shaft's lineal pattern stresses the direction of the plane in which it has been inserted, affirms the angle of its juncture with the main body of the building, and is a variation of the transparent motif of the auxiliary staircase which finishes the building on the east. Window frames that appear fragmentarily through the open-work parasols determine the reticulated structure. A lineal avalanche defines the shape of the museum, extolling the horizontality of its bulk and the depth of shade produced by the eaves. All these elements seem to assert that "the origin of art," as Josef Albers would say, "is found in the difference between the physical fact and the psychic effect," and "that the content of art is the visual formation of our reaction to life, and the measure of art the relationship between effort and effect."[19]

83. *Ciudad Universitaria, School of Architecture, plan, ground floor.*

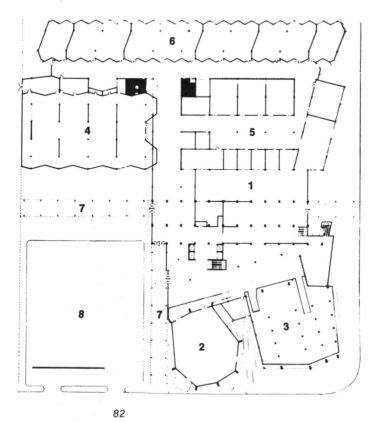

1. Cafeteria
2. Auditorium
3. Museum and exhibition hall
4. Construction workshops
5. Visual design workshops
6. Composition workshops
7. Covered corridors
8. Parking

MONUMENTAL
ARCHITECTURE

EMILIO Duhart's United Nations building at Vitacura, a suburb of Santiago de Chile, is the clearest embodiment of so-called monumental architecture (*Figs. 84–89*). It has become the fashion in architectural journals to heap abundant scorn on such buildings. Nevertheless, it remains a fact that, no matter what we do, certain buildings because of their character or location will always acquire a landmark quality. This is what Duhart accepted as a starting point when he defined his building as a "House of Nations," and as a "monumental, visible expression of spiritual and social endeavours."[20]

Obviously, the closed form of the whole is intended to affirm categorically the joint effort of the Latin American nations which contribute to E.C.L.A. (Economic Council for Latin America), U.N.E.S.C.O., and other organizations. The Latin American past, its sun myths and obsessions with water are not absent, but the building's implicit technical achievement shows that no one is turning his back to the future. In recognition of the contribution of the people who made the building, the workers' handprints were impressed in the entrance wall.

The building, located on the left bank of the Mapocho River, will be the focal point of the future Park of the Americas. The San Cristobal and Manquehue hills surround the river basin; the Andes rise in the distance. One immediately perceives that they were present in Duhart's imagination from the first. To the cosmic energy of the Andes, he opposes the neat geometry of square form, but the sense of this dialogue becomes apparent only once one has passed through the entrance gate and proceeded toward the building. The building has been placed slightly obliquely in relation to the entrance to Hammarskjold Avenue—14° east of north—not only to catch the prevailing south-southwest afternoon breeze and to balance the sun control of the façades, but also to contrast the rising form of the Snail Shell (main conference hall) to the V-cleft body of the Manquehue.

An asymmetrical oval pool is placed before the building; vehicular traffic circulates around it and pedestrians may cross it over a straight bridge. It is fed from a rainwater reservoir north of the building by an open channel through the central court, and acts as a cooling tower for the air-conditioning system. The square office building or Ring, 100 meters by 100 meters, encircles a large central patio containing the buildings common to all the organiza-

84. *Emilio Duhart: U.N. building, Santiago, Chile, 1966, aerial view.*

85. *U.N. building, southern façade. In the background, the Andes.*

86. *U.N. building, Snail Shell (conference hall) and bridge.*

87. *U.N. building, entrance patio.*

tions, which are linked to the Ring by pedestrian bridges. The Ring, bold and simple in appearance, has been raised above the ground level, enabling the patio space to expand under its protective shadow. The central group is composed of the Nucleus, which houses halls, restaurant services, and so forth, the Snail Shell, and the Diamond or assembly hall which is as yet unbuilt.

Duhart's solution of the structure of these units is implied in the role he has attributed to each of them. The Ring's aerial rhythmic and repetitious quality is opposed to the central system's gravitational emphasis. Heavy forms are thus given to the permanent character of the consulting assemblies, and the lighter, more flexible forms to the changing tasks of the organizational infrastructure. The suspended structure of the Ring was designed to absorb earthquake movements almost entirely. A pair of edge beams, which run around the Ring and rest on articulated joints on four columns per side, are cantilevered at the four corners. A system of precast transversal beams enable the floor slab to be suspended.

The great space within the helicoidal Snail Shell is topped by a white fiberglass inverted saucer, the Moon, which can be raised or lowered. It serves as both a sound deflector and a lighting feature. Two exterior heliostats reflect sun rays through a porthole on the northern side onto a small moveable mirror concealed between the outer and inner walls of the cone, and from there onto the Moon which diffuses natural light without dazzle or glare. Artificial light is also projected onto the Moon by a device hidden in the center of the hall.

88. *U.N. building, western façade.*

Duhart's building shows once more that concrete is the basic material used throughout Latin America; this has been the case for many years and will continue to be so. In the absence of cheap steel for frames, it is the structural material par excellence; through the years Latin Americans have become very skilled with it and are ranked as its most talented users. In a way this links recent Latin American architecture to Le Corbusier's experience from Marseilles on. His influence is indisputable, and greater in Latin America than that of any of the other "form-givers." However, this is reflected in basic attitudes more than in finished forms.

The Benedictine Monastery Church at Las Condes, near Santiago, by the Brothers Martín and Gabriel (*Figs. 90–93*) confirms the above. The way the chapel closes the access road may be derived from La Tourette, but the handling of the inner space and the resulting outer irregular geometry of sharp-edged cubes intersecting each other is wholly original. Schematically, the chapel is composed of two cubes of different heights, placed diagonally to each other and intersected at their angles in the center of the total layout. Here the altar has been placed. Sunlight, admitted through a vertical slit, through horizontal skylights, or below a suspended wall, leads the worshiper to the altar, and as the sun follows its course it bathes the rough white concrete walls with changing intensity and color.

89. *U.N. building, Snail Shell with Moon.*

90. *Brothers Martín and Gabriel: Benedictine Monastery Church, Las Condes, Chile, 1965, entrance.*

91. *Benedictine Monastery Church, overlooking valley.*

92. *Benedictine Monastery Church, interior.*

93. *Benedictine Monastery Church, entrance ramp.*

Nelson Bayardo's columbarium at the Northern Cemetery of Montevideo (*Figs. 94–96*) is another example in the same direction. Here again a raised volume, strongly and simply defined on the exterior, encircles a patio. The framework of the structural supports has impressed its rough texture on the parietal concrete box and so become identified with it. The raised volume which acts as a portico is the entrance to the sunken patio. Its shadow contrasts with the luminosity of the patio which has been designed as a place of meeting and meditation. From here an echeloned ramp ascends toward the open upper gallery, the urn depository itself. The abstract nakedness of great construction mural by Edwin Studer, which accompanies this solemn movement, has an elegiac dignity which presides over the whole building.

In Uruguay, Le Corbusier's influence has merged with two national trends which are manifested in all of the nation's leading works, the heritage of Julio Vilamajó and Joaquín Torres García. This is evident not only in Bayardo's work, but also in Mario Payssé Reyes' house at Carrasco (*Fig. 97*) and in his later building, the Banco de la República in Punta del Este (*Fig. 98*).

94. *Nelson Bayardo: Columbarium, Northern Cemetery, Montevideo, Uruguay, 1962, façade.*

95. *Columbarium, patio and entrance.*

96. *Columbarium, patio, ramp, and mural.*

97. *Mario Payssé Reyes: Private house, Carrasco, Uruguay, 1958, patio.*

98. *Mario Payssé Reyes: Banco de la República, Punta del Este, Uruguay, 1962.*

THE NEW GENERATION

NEW directions may originate in the works of young architects between about thirty-five and forty-five years of age, such as Clorindo
Testa, Vittorio Garatti, Fernando Salinas, Ricardo Porro, Nelson
Bayardo, and Claudio Caveri. Or they may have their origin in
the works of an older master born at the turn of the century such
as Carlos Raúl Villanueva, in those of a middle-aged, world-famous
creator such as Félix Candela, or in the activity of talented men who
are almost ignored outside their own country, as may be the case
with Emilio Duhart, Eladio Dieste, and the team of Carlos Bresciani,
Hector Valdés, Fernando Castillo, and Carlos G. Huidobro, all in
their early fifties. All these men are contributing toward new developments. It is difficult to say particularly where one should look in
order to know what will take place tomorrow. Some architects, such
as Louis Kahn and Villanueva, for example, begin to produce their
truly significant works very late in life; others meet with success
very early and fade later on when one would expect their decisive
works.

As history has proven, the future is unpredictable. It is logical,
though, that the younger men will have to bear most of the burden
of the challenging situation and changing circumstances of the near
future, and that from these quarters one should expect the most
vital responses, even while accepting that architecture is the product
of a dialogue between generations. This section will therefore be
devoted entirely to the younger generation.

In Latin America, as in the rest of the world, an architect
rarely finds important opportunities before he is thirty-five. The case
of Cuba, where a group of very young architects completely control
the situation, is exceptional, although not surprising in a country
where revolutionary political leadership was from the beginning in
the hands of youthful activists. Granted that the competition may not
be as intense as in Europe or the United States, giant firms the size
of Skidmore, Owings, and Merrill are nonexistent, the number of
interesting opportunities is smaller, and the technical limitations
often imply a narrower range of possibilities.

Every generation must confront the previous one. It is interesting
to examine the attitude of the new generation toward older masters
such as Le Corbusier, who seems to have had an unchallenged
authority in Latin American architecture, and to analyze the trend
of thought and action being followed by the younger architects.

If one looks at Rogelio Salmona's and Hernan Vieco's work, it seems that Le Corbusier's influence may be fading. Their Marulandia housing development in Bogotá (*Figs. 99–102*), whose echeloned schema gives each apartment a view of the Andes and whose recessive diagonal treatment of the eastern façades reflects the decreasing size of the higher apartments, is more related to some of the recent Spanish work, such as that by José Martorell and Oriol Bohigas, than to Le Corbusier's. Although the use of local brick and corrugated asbestos cement sheets may seem brutal at first, of all the masters it is certainly Alvar Aalto, if anyone, whose effect is present here.

The first stages of the project, sponsored by the Fundación Cristiana de la Vivienda, a private agency, to accommodate medium-

99. *Rogelio Salmona and Hernan Vieco: Marulandia housing development, Bogotá, Colombia, 1966.*

high income families, were built in 1965–66. The unit consists of 150 apartments in six buildings which converge toward the center of the site, where there is a playground for children, a local shop, and a community hall. Aside from allowing each household a panoramic view of the mountain chain that surrounds Bogotá, this radial layout permits a concentration of daily activities.

Each building is composed of four, five, or six sections, which contain the main staircase and five apartment units each. The units are superimposed so that each uses as a terrace part of the roof of the apartment below. This overlapping increases the surface of the façade and therefore the area exposed to the sun.

The average area of the units is 85 square meters. As they

100. *Marulandia housing development.*

are echeloned along the hypotenuse of the triangle from which they originate, the plan of the main hall and the number of bedrooms vary. The design of the whole complex was based on a module (1.08 by 1.32 meters), allowing the concrete slab and the structure to be prefabricated.

To return to Le Corbusier, he seems to have played an important role in the decline of Brazilian vernacular architecture, which was, after all, a child of his. As early as 1960 even Oscar Niemeyer had abandoned reinforced concrete, curving forms in his project for the Development Palace at Brasilia.[21] Glauco Campelo, a young architect working with him in Brasilia at the time, avoided the usual vernacular in his S. Kubitschek rehabilitation center in Brasilia 1960, linking his work instead with the Miesian tradition, although in a coarser way. The winning project for the Peugeot office building competition at Buenos Aires, by Roberto Aflalo, Plinio Croce, Gian Carlo Gasperini of Brazil, and Eduardo Saurez, an Argentine working in São Paulo, also ignored the usual grammar in favor of Mies. A general reaction appeared to be developing against the preceding forms, which were believed to be exhausted.

However, when one looks at the D. Toledo house in Piracicaba, São Paulo (*Figs. 103–104*), by Joaquim Guedes, Brazil's most outstanding representative of the young generation, it seems that the inspiration for this reaction might have risen out of a tough interpretation of Le Corbusier's late works, as was the case with the new

101. *Marulandia housing development.*

102. *Marulandia housing development, plan.*

103. *Joaquim Guedes: D. Toledo house, Piracicaba, São Paulo, Brazil, 1963, rear view.*

104. *D. Toledo house, living room.*

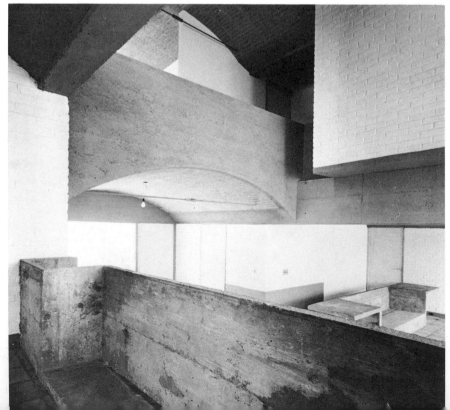

brutalism in Europe. Curiously enough then, both Mies and Le Corbusier may be regarded as the fountainheads of the new directions in Brazil around 1960, as in England.

The architectural interregnum that followed Niemeyer's political disgrace, Reidy's death, and the wave of criticism over Brasilia opened the way for a new experience. By 1955 Guedes was already working on what he termed a "crude and brutal construction concerned with economics in its wider sense and interested in formulating an un-aesthetic and anti-academic attitude." He rejected "the formalism which hovered over our architecture" and thought that "the solutions in the accepted taste were light, opportunistic, and in the end, ignored Brazil because of a methodological incompatibility."[22]

Guedes, unlike others, is not interested in the works of Yona Friedman or in Archigram, for he believes it is useless "to dream of homes for the day when the private property of urban land will have disappeared. Will the private house then have a meaning? What will the collective residence require? There is an insurmountable difficulty. It is possible to imagine spaces, machines and speeds for the year 2001. But it is very difficult to imagine what man will become, what a family will look like and what kind of social relations we will have. In a future which promises to change that much, is it not necessary to admit that man will undergo profound changes? My interest lies in the approaching battle which is the condition of tomorrow's victory. Our reality is today. Others will make the reality tomorrow, it will be their duty and they will confront it with more knowledge. Incidentally, it seems rather pretentious to determine the world of those who are not yet born while we seem unable to do anything with our own."[23] This does not mean that Guedes renounces change and rejects utopia completely; he himself admits that "in planning I tend toward radical solutions which bring me to attitudes very close to utopia." In 1956, for example, he proposed a linear and vertical city for Brasilia, which would have been served by a rapid transit system of unlimited growth potential. The project emerged less as a genuine, final proposal than as a rejection of the neighborhood unit system, of the garden city, the "cité naturelle," the satellite town, the new town, and the "policité" schemes. It was immediately turned down by the jury since, according to the urban program, Brasilia's population was not to exceed 600,000 and the city was to be conceived as a specialized administrative complex.

However, this rejection of established models should not be interpreted as a sterile negation. It is increasingly felt that the models proposed by affluent societies are of little or no use in Latin America. We have seen above ("Urban Utopia and Reality") how the barriada experience has opened the way for a new approach based on what may be termed a crude realism. The new generation has varying attitudes toward the barriada experience, but in general it is entirely committed to the sense of public participation and design for change that are implicit in the experience. Although Guedes, with the rest of the younger architects, would like to devote himself to planning and public housing, most of his work consists of private houses. One of his first interesting works, the Cunha Lima house at Pacaembú, São Paulo (*Fig. 105*), is set on a steep slope and juts over an open terrace with swimming pool; thus resorting to structural acrobatics which are not alien to the Brazilian vernacular. However, the resulting form seems entirely committed to the handling of space in a very small lot, out of which the architect has taken all possible advantages. The living area, raised from the ground and linked to the street, is supported by four central pillars which spread out to support the heavier planes, and join the volume to the ground.

The F. Landi house at Butantan, São Paulo (*Figs. 106–107*), a good example of the angry stick-to-the-facts attitude which seems prevalent among the new generation, shows that Guedes is on his own and is no longer depending on other form-givers. It is a rigorous and coarse synthesis in concrete, brick, corrugated asbestos sheets, and glass, which does not indulge in any of the sweet formulas of

105. *Joaquim Guedes: Cunha Lima house, Pacaembú, São Paulo, Brazil, 1958, street façade.*

106. *Joaquim Guedes and others: F. Landi house, Butantan, São Paulo, 1966, façade.*

107. *F. Landi house, garden façade.*

the soft Brazilian vernacular. Among his other works may be mentioned the W. P. Pereira house at Morumbi (*Fig. 108*); the Costa Neto house at Pacaembú, in which the inner space has been resolved through an interplay of the different levels (*Fig. 109*); the forum at Itapira in collaboration with J. C. de Mello and H. Penteado (*Fig. 110*); and the projects for the J. Breyton house at Vila Maricuna (1965), for the Colegio Salesiano Sao José at Sorocaba (1967), and for the Escola Salesiana at Campinas (1965). That the direction of his more recent works has some following in Brazil is evident from the houses of Sergio Ferro and Rodrigo Lefèvre at Itaim and Butantan.

Since 1955 a process similar to that in Brazil has been taking place in Argentina, though with different details and in a different context. The Black Beauty horse farm in the province of Buenos Aires, by Leonardo Aizemberg and José Rey Pastor (*Fig. 111*), followed the grammar of Gerrit Thomas Rietveld's Schroeder house (Utrecht, 1924) in attempting a bold analysis of the individual architectural elements. In the already mentioned Iglesia Nuestra Señora de Fátima (*Figs. 60–61*) two other young architects, Claudio Caveri and Eduardo Ellis, sought an elementary sense of materials. This search for immediacy and directness, however, concealed a self-consciousness that permeates most of the thought and action of the younger generation and sometimes becomes evident in over-design, as may be the case with Oscar Molinos' Soldatti house at Martinez (*Fig. 112*), or of studied elegance, as in Horacio Baliero's

108. *Joaquim Guedes and others: W. P. Pereira house, Morumbi, São Paulo, Brazil, 1968, façade.*

109. *Joaquim Guedes: Costa Neto house, Pacaembú, São Paulo, Brazil, 1961, living room.*

110. *Joaquim Guedes, with J. C. de Mello and H. Penteado: Forum, Itapira, São Paulo, Brazil, 1958, detail of side façade.*

111. *Leonardo Aizemberg and José Rey Pastor: Black Beauty horse farm, Ituzaingo, province of Buenos Aires, Argentina, 1954.*

112. *Oscar Molinos: Soldatti house, Martinez, province of Buenos Aires, Argentina, 1962, street façade.*

113. *Horacio Baliero and C. C. de Baliero: Israeli Panthéon, Cemetery, Mar del Plata, Argentina, 1965.*

and C. C. de Baliero's Israeli Pantheon at the Mar del Plata Cemetery (*Fig. 113*). Form remains an important consideration for the new generation, although it is often denied or repressed under false justifications of functional needs such as waterproof construction, or is generally rejected as formalism. What is really meant is not so much that form is unimportant, but that it should be conceived in another context.

The work of Clorindo Testa, the leading representative of the younger Argentine generation, may clarify some aspects of the change that has been taking place. From the soft grammar of his early works in the early fifties, he turned to a bold, 180-meter-long block in his Provincial Government House at Santa Rosa, La Pampa (*Fig. 114*), which he worked out in terms of a three-dimensional, sun-control façade, open well-like halls, and two-story-high peripheral galleries. The bus terminal across from the Government House em-

114. *Clorindo Testa with Francisco Rossi, Augusto Gaido, and Boris Dabinovic: Provincial Government House, Santa Rosa, La Pampa, Argentina, 1956–63.*

phasizes the sole, sun-protecting function of the umbrellas, under which a rough brick and *béton brut* succession of walls houses areas such as the waiting room, ticket office, bar, and open waiting area (*Fig. 115*).

Testa's headquarters of the Bank of London and South America, discussed above, obviously moves away from new brutalist coarseness. This direction becomes clearer yet in the Harrods branch of the same bank at Buenos Aires (*Figs. 116–117*). Yet here the adjustment of the moveable panels, and the detailing in general, show that none of the earlier directness has been lost. The accidental quality of joints, ducts, or service equipment is emphasized, not hidden or sublimated under an undifferentiated grammar, and the work's totality arises out of the specificity of each situation. This contradicts one of the basic assumptions of both academic and Bauhaus orthodoxy, that the part is subordinate to the pre-established order of the whole.

115. Clorindo Testa with Francisco Rossi, Augusto Gaido, and Boris Dabinovic: Bus terminal, Santa Rosa, La Pampa, Argentina, 1956–61.

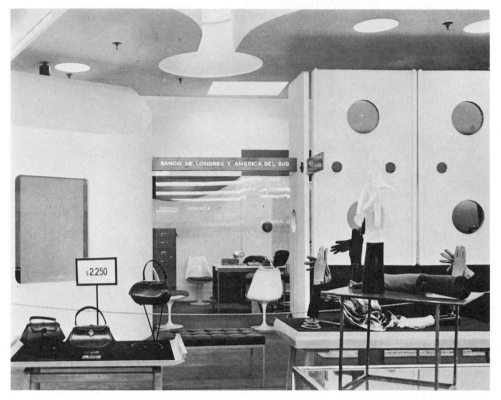

116. *Clorindo Testa, Santiago Sanchez Elia, Federico Peralta Ramos, and Alfredo Agostini (S.E.P.R.A.): Bank of London and South America, Harrod's branch, Buenos Aires, Argentina, 1962–64, entrance.*

117. *Bank of London and South America, Harrod's branch, counters.*

In his Ollé Perez house at Punta Ballena, Uruguay, Juan M. Borthagaray does not seem to try "to create order out of the desperate confusion of our time," as would be the wish of Mies, his mentor, but to accommodate the circumstantial realities of a program to a given site (*Fig. 118*). He himself states that the house was the result of "a search for Mannerist ambivalence which ignores classical purity, and accepts contradiction in order to integrate itself in the casuistry of life."[24]

Exceptions and circumstances are exactly what the new generation is trying to include in its work, because it believes that unless "the vagaries of the user, which bring an architectural pattern to life" are taken into account, no significative environment will ever be created.[25] This is considered valid on both the architectural and the urban levels.

It is felt that the architect's job is to create an infrastructural reality into which the individual user would be able to plug-in the honky-tonk of his choice. Instead of conceiving their work as a totality, which excludes the participation of the public, the younger architects are exploring new approaches. Because they feel that

118. *Juan M. Borthagaray: Ollé Perez house, Punta Ballena, Uruguay, 1966, entrance façade.*

119. *Jorge Erbin, M. Baudizzone, A. Varas, and J. Lestard: Gonzalez Porto bookstore, Buenos Aires, Argentina, 1968, entrance.*

participationism in time is bound to introduce intriguing solecisms, they are experimenting with them now. This does not lead us to a picturesqueness of the kind proposed almost twenty years ago by Nikolaus Pevsner and *The Architectural Review*. The younger architects have in the main discarded the modern orthodox rejection of honky-tonk. They intend either to integrate existing honky-tonk as *objects trouvés*, or to create a honky-tonk of their own, which after all is what Pop Art is all about.

Seriousness, implying puritanical orderliness, is considered rather boring and inconsistent with the popular aims of today's architecture. This attitude is clearly visible in the Gonzalez Porto bookstore in Buenos Aires, by Jorge Erbin, M. Baudizzone, A. Varas, and J. Lestard (*Figs. 119–120*). It is a typical example of the so-called consumer architecture favored by many younger architects, particularly in Argentina, a country with a relatively high per capita income. This does not mean, however, that these architects agree with the social patterns of behavior of the "affluent society."

On the one hand, the pure consumer attitude is viewed as of dubious or negative moral value, especially in countries whose serious problems of development require a higher rate of saving. It is also felt, in the context of the existing economic and social structure, that promoting a consumer attitude only favors in the end a wider control of society by those groups that already hold the power of decision in their hands. On the other hand, consumer

120. *Gonzalez Porto bookstore, interior.*

architecture and consumption in general is considered as a non-aristocratic social reality, and as a possibility of creating an authentic popular culture and environment. A truly Pop attitude must necessarily avoid the distinction, usually emphasized by the purists, between architecture and the environment.

The hemispherical marquee of the Gonzalez Porto bookstore pops out into the Avenida de Mayo without trying to impose silence on the street's chaos of neon, but on the contrary taking advantage of its vital atmosphere. The cylindrical acrylic entrance sucks one into the store. Acrylic sheets have been visibly adjusted with screws. The bare steel structure irrupts suddenly, its supporting function having been rather obscured by its visual context. It is therefore not surprising that the close relation between structure and space, which in the past has been considered of paramount importance, may in some cases be almost nonexistent. Services, and their integration in an architectural language, seem to be the central preoccupation. Structure is often imagined as an envelope of services, or as having additional functions beyond its purely structural one.

The dictum that form follows function has been subjected to strong *de facto* criticism, but this does not imply that all interdependence has been eliminated. When the architect must deal with multifunctional spaces and forms—as is nearly always the case—it is believed that the theory of functionalism, in its simplified version, does not explain the true process through which a work is evolved. In fact, architects do not deduct an architectural image from an organigram, but themselves propose an initial formal synthesis which they afterward try to develop and adjust. The process of design is thus a continual adjustment of the initial idea to circumstantial reality. If a satisfactory adjustment cannot be made, the architect—with this experience in mind—will try to find another image which may or may not resist the following stage of development. Thus form is inevitably a "starting" point, a fact which no amount of scorn can obscure.

Space is implicit in form, and spatial organization seems to be one of the basic concerns of the new architecture. The treatment of inner space as a complex reality is evident not only in the Bank of London but also in the Cuban pavilion at Expo '67 (*Figs. 66–68*), the Marulandia housing development (*Figs. 99–102*), and the Cunha Lima house (*Fig. 105*). Space is imagined not only in terms of its visual reality but in terms of the existential experience of it.

Justo Solsona's recent remodeling of the Banco Municipal in Buenos Aires exemplifies the above considerations (*Figs. 121–122*). Although the building chosen to accommodate the bank facilities was an old store built at the beginning of this century, the architect had no trouble turning it into what he thought a bank should be. He left the exterior almost untouched and pulled down the interior except the floors, tearing down the Beaux-Arts decoration and exposing

121. *Justo Solsona: Banco Municipal, Buenos Aires, Argentina, 1968.*

the steel structure. Efficiency, not pomposity, is expected in banks today, and their architecture should reflect this.

The four-level banking hall creates a unified space in which improvised and accidental episodes are integrated. The floors, walls, and ceiling are wrapped with orange-amber-colored glass bricks lit from behind. Within this box are freely displayed steel-framed, white-painted mezzanines linked by bridges and stairs. The wrapping wall is pierced so that onlookers can watch what is happening from hanging balconies. Thus the pedestrian street becomes part of the bank, and vice-versa. In the upper management floors, colored glass partitions and wall-to-wall carpeted flooring create an atmosphere of quiet elegance.

This unifying wrapping treatment has many antecedents in Solsona's work, including the way in which the tile roof of his Sierchuck house continues down as a wall (*Fig. 123*). Set on a steep slope, the house has its street entrance at an intermediate level, as does Guedes' Cunha Lima house. The roof follows the movement of

122. *Banco Municipal, banking hall.*

123. *Justo Solsona: Sierchuck house, province of Buenos Aires, Argentina, 1960.*

the topography, and although it envelopes the interior space, with its intricate organization as a whole, it acknowledges the exterior demands of the site and view, which directed the house's orientation with its back to the street. The idea appears again in another context in the FATE building in which the continuity of the surface treatment has been enriched by the joints, which show the fragmented constructional system used to cover the façade (*Fig. 124*).

The same principle may be found in Solsona's project for the National Library at Buenos Aires, which won second prize in the 1962 national competition. Although the winning project by Clorindo Testa, Alicia Cazzaniga de Bullrich, and Francisco Bullrich may seem to

124. *Justo Solsona: FATE building, Buenos Aires, Argentina, 1966.*

some critics like an architectural student's project, it is a design seriously intended for construction (*Fig. 125*). Whether it is a putative resurrection of heroic modernism or a new trend on its own, is something I cannot say. It is shown here mainly for the reader to know the author's activity as a practicing architect.

I have tried to demonstrate that, in spite of its specificity, Latin American architecture is part of world architecture; proof of this is that architects south of the Rio Grande have been exchanging ideas with architects of other continents. I hope this book will bear witness to the meaning and value of Latin American architects' own contribution.

125. *Clorindo Testa, Alicia Cazzaniga de Bullrich, and Francisco Bullrich: National Library, Buenos Aires, Argentina, 1962, model.*

NOTES

1. Jorge E. Hardoy, *Las Ciudades Precolombinas* (Buenos Aires: Infinito, 1965).
2. Richard Morse, "Some Characteristics of Latin American Urban History," *American Historical Review*, LXVII (January 2, 1962), 317–338.
3. The term *Porfirismo* is derived from the name of Porfirio Diaz, president of Mexico from 1876–1911, who was ousted during the revolutionary movement headed by Francisco Madero. His administration was marked by adaptation to European patterns of behavior and by a lack of social concern.
4. Alejandro Christophersen, "Nuevos Rumbos," *Revista de Arquitectura* (Buenos Aires, July, 1915), p. 7.
5. *Estado Novo* (new state) is the usual designation of President Getulio Vargas' rule (1934–46).
6. *Hypnerotomachia Poliphili*, a dream allegory written around 1467 by Francesco Colonna under the pseudonym Poliphilus, played a considerable part in gradually awakening humanist interest in classical gardens.
7. Wilhelm Worringer, *Form in Gothic* (New York: Schocken, 1964), pp. 37ff. (Originally published as *Formprobleme der Gotik* [Munich: Piper Verlag, 1911].)
8. Quoted in *Nuestra Arquitectura* (Buenos Aires, June, 1939), leaflet.
9. Bonet's house for Rafael Alberti (Punta del Este, 1946) and his Cuatrecasas house (Punta Ballena, 1947), among other Argentine works of the period, are similar more to Le Corbusier's house at Mathes (1935) and his Maison Mandrot (1931) than to other works by him. It is revealing that Le Corbusier never included the house at Mathes in his *Oeuvres Complètes*. (Alfred Roth, *La Nouvelle Architecture* [Zurich: Les Editions d'Architecture Erlenbach, 1947], p. 17.)
10. Le Corbusier, *Oeuvres Complètes 1938–1946* (Zurich: Les Editions d'Architecture Erlenbach, 1946), p. 13.
11. Hardoy's and Kurchan's apartment at Virrey del Pino 2664 was conceived as a transitional urban unit, a first step toward a Ville Radieuse. Basically planned as a middle income apartment, it was intended to test living standards for this housing bracket.
12. Le Corbusier, *op. cit.*, p. 118.
13. Giulio Carlo Argan, *Progetto e Destino* (Milan: Il Saggiatore, 1965), p. 63ff.
14. From 1954–1958 the Perez Jimenez regime built in Caracas 85 super-blocks and 68 four-story blocks. In 1959, after the downfall of the Jimenez administration, the Centro Interamericano de Vivienda y Planeamiento (C.I.N.V.A.) evaluated the program. At the time these buildings housed 160,000 people, or 12 per cent of the city's population, in 17,399 apartment units. The average construction cost for each unit was $10,000, and monthly maintenance costs in 1959 were $53.44. These costs were far too high for the average income of the occupants. The housing conditions bordered on social chaos: elevators had broken down, interior staircases were filthy, violence in the corridors exceeded

all bounds. Following recommendations of the C.I.N.V.A. study, groups of social workers began pilot projects, and the situation has improved although much remains to be done. ("Mass Urban Re-housing Problems," *Architectural Design*, XXXIII [London, August, 1963], 373; and Sibyl Moholy-Nagy, *Carlos Raúl Villanueva and the Architecture of Venezuela* [New York, 1964], pp. 141ff.)

15. John Turner, Catherine S. Turner, Patrick P. Crooke, "Dwelling Resources in South America: Conclusions," *Architectural Design*, XXXIII (London, August, 1963), 389ff.

16. Juan Pablo Bonta, *Eladio Dieste* (Buenos Aires: Instituto de Arte Americano e Investigaciones Estéticas, 1963), pp. 13ff.

17. *Ibid.*

18. J. M. Richards "Report from Cuba," *Architectural Review*, CXXXV (London, March, 1964), 222.

19. Josef Albers, *Nueva Vision*, No. 8 (Buenos Aires, 1955), p. 9.

20. Emilio Duhart, "Edifico de Naciones Unidas," AUCA, No. 3 (Santiago, 1966), p. 30.

21. "Niemeyer—Constructivist?" *Architectural Review*, CXXIX (London, March, 1961), 149.

22. Joaquim Guedes, "Depoimiento," *Acropole*, No. 347 (São Paulo, February, 1968), p. 14.

23. *Ibid.*

24. Juan M. Borthagaray, "Casa Pérez," *Summa*, No. 14 (Buenos Aires, December, 1968), p. 23.

25. Theo Crosby, *Architecture: City Sense* (New York: Reinhold, 1965), p. 17.

BIBLIOGRAPHY

Books

Bardi, Pietro Maria. *Tropical Gardens of Burle Marx*. New York: Reinhold, 1964.

Bonta, Juan Pablo. *Eladio Dieste*. Buenos Aires, 1963.

Bullrich, Francisco. *Arquitectura Argentina Contemporánea*. Buenos Aires, 1963.

Candela, Félix. "Strutture e Strutturalismo" *Casabella* (Milan), October, 1959.

Cetto, Max. *Moderne Architektur in Mexico*. Stuttgart: Verlag Hatje, 1961.

Damaz, Paul E. *Art in Latin American Architecture*. New York: Reinhold, 1956.

Franck, Klaus. *Eduardo Affonso Reidy. Works and Projects*. New York: Praeger, 1960.

Goodwin, Philip L. and Elizabeth Mock. *Brazil Builds*. New York: The Museum of Modern Art, 1943.

Hitchcock, Henry-Russell. *Latin American Architecture Since 1945*. New York: The Museum of Modern Art, 1955.

Mindlin, Henrique E. *Modern Architecture in Brazil*. New York: Reinhold, 1956.

Moholy-Nagy, Sibyl. *Carlos Raúl Villanueva and the Architecture of Venezuela*. New York: Praeger, 1964.

Papadaky, Stamo. *Oscar Niemeyer*. New York: Braziller, 1960.

Papadaky, Stamo. *Oscar Niemeyer. Works in Progress*. New York: Reinhold, 1956.

Segre, Roberto. *La Arquitectura de la Revolución Cubana*. Montevideo: Universidad de la Republica, 1968.

Serge, Roberto and G. Peani. "Saggi sull Argentina," *Casabella* (Milan), May, 1964.

Journals

Acosta, Wladimiro, "Villa à la Falda," *L'Architecture d'Aujourd'hui* (June, 1948), p. 64.

"Brazil" (special issue), *Architectural Forum*, LXXXVII (November, 1947).

"Brésil" (special issue), *L'Architecture d'Aujourd'hui* (September, 1947). Introduction by Lúcio Costa.

"Brésil" (special issue), *L'Architecture d'Aujourd'hui* (August, 1952).

Catalano, Eduard F., *et al.*, "Bloc à Rio de la Plata," *L'Architecture d'Aujourd'hui* (September, 1950), p. 14.

————, "Théâtre Auditorium de Buenos Aires," *L'Architecture d'Aujourd'hui* (May, 1949), p. 28.

Crease, David, "Progress in Brasilia," *Architectural Review*, CXXXII (April, 1962), 257.

"18 Houses by Mexican Architects," *Architectural Forum* (August, 1951).

"Mass Urban Re-housing Problems," *Architectural Design*, XXXIII (August, 1963), 373.

"Mexique" (special issue), *L'Architecture d'Aujourd'hui* (October, 1958).

Moholy-Nagy, Sibyl, "Some Aspects of Latin American Architecture," *Progressive Architecture*, XLI (April, 1960), 135.

Nicholson, Irene, "Mexican Newsletter," *Architectural Review*, CXXX (London, August, 1961), 101–103.

Pani, Mario, *et al.*, *"Centre Urbain* 'President Aleman,' Mexico," *L'Architecture d'Aujourd'hui* (September, 1950), p. 2.

Paulsson, Gregory, *et al.*, "In Search of a New Monumentality: A Symposium," *Architectural Review*, CIV (September, 1948). Participants included Henry-Russell Hitchcock, William Halford, Sigfried Giedion, Walter Gropius, Lúcio Costa, and Alfred Roth.

Repossini, Maurice, and Alberti Siperman, "Immeubles d'Appartements à Buenos Aires," *L'Architecture d'Aujourd'hui* (September, 1950), p. 15.

"Report on Brazil," *Architectural Review*, CXVI (October, 1954).

Richards, J. M., "Report from Cuba," *Architectural Review*, CXXXI (March, 1962), 222.

Smith, C. Ray, "After Corbu, What's Happening?," *Progressive Architecture*, XLVII (September, 1966), 140.

Villanueva, Carlos Raúl, "Nouvelle Unités Residentielles au Venezuela," *L'Architecture d'Aujourd'hui* (September, 1950), p. 8.

Vivanco, Jorge, *et al.*, "Groupe de Quatre Pavillons à Martinez," *L'Architecture d'Aujourd'hui* (June, 1948).

Williams, Amancio, and Delfinia G. de Williams, "Residence à Mar del Plata," *L'Architecture d'Aujourd'hui* (June, 1948), p. 62.

Zevi, Bruno, "Brasilia come LEUR," *Architettura* (January, 1961).

———, "Inchiesta su Brasilia," *Architettura* (January, 1960).

The principal Latin American journals are: *Acropole* (São Paulo, Brazil); *ADEM: Arquitectos de Mexico* (Mexico City, Mexico); *Arquitectura* (Havana, Cuba); *AUCA* (Santiago, Chile); *El Arquitecto Peruano* (Lima, Peru); *Integral* (Caracas, Venezuela); *Proa, Urbanismo, Arquitectura, Industrias* (Bogotá, Colombia); *Revista de la Facultad de Arquitectura* (Montevideo, Uruguay); *Summa: Revista de Arquitectura, Technologia y Diseño* (Buenos Aires, Argentina).

INDEX

Aalto, Alvar, 94
Aflalo, Roberto, 96
  Peugeot office building (Buenos
    Aires), 96
Agostini, Alfredo, 49
  Bank of London and South
    America, Harrod's branch
    (Buenos Aires), 107, 112; *Figs.*
    116–117
  Bank of London and South
    America, headquarters (Buenos
    Aires), 49, 51–52, 54, 112; *Figs.*
    32–37
Aizemberg, Leonardo, 102
  Black Beauty horse farm
    (Ituzaingo, Arg.), 102; *Fig.* 111
Albers, Josef, 82
Alvarez, Augusto, 54
Antunes Ribeiro, Paulo, 26
Archigram, 99
Architectural Review, 111
Argentina, 13, 15–16, 19–20, 30–32,
  35, 44, 49, 51–52, 54, 62, 96, 102,
  106–107, 111–112, 114, 116–117;
  Figs. 1–2, 15–17, 32–37, 60–61,
  111–117, 119–125
Arp, Hans, 27, 77
Art, Nouveau, 15
Asplund, Gunnar, 21
Austral group, 20–21, 30–31
  Belgrano housing development
    (Buenos Aires), 30

Baliero, C. C. de, 106
  Israeli Panthéon, Cemetery (Mar
    del Plata, Arg.), 106; *Fig.* 113
Baliero, Horacio, 102
  Israeli Panthéon, Cemetery (Mar
    del Plata, Arg.), 106; *Fig.* 113
Baroni, Sergio
  Cuban pavilion, Expo '67
    (Montreal), 70, 112; *Figs.* 66–68
Baudizzone, M., 111
  Gonzales Porto bookstore (Buenos
    Aires), 111–112; *Figs.* 119–120
Bauhaus, 28, 49, 107
Bayardo, Nelson, 90, 93
  Columbarium, Northern Cemetery
    (Montevideo), 90; *Figs.* 94–96
Bermudez, Guido, 41
  Cerro Piloto housing development
    (Caracas), 41, 43; *Fig.* 26

El Paraiso housing development
    (Caracas), 41, 43
23 de Enero housing development
    (Caracas), 41, 43; *Figs.* 24–25
Bernardes, Sergio, 26
Boari, Adamo, 15
  Marulandia housing development
    (Salmona and Vieco), 94–96,
    112; *Figs.* 99–102
  Palacio de Bellas Artes (Mexico
    City), 15
Bohigas, Oriol, 94
Bolivia, 13–14
Bonet, Antonio, 30
  Berlingieri house (Punta Ballena,
    Ur.), 30; *Fig.* 13
  La Solana del Mar (Punta Ballena,
    Ur.), 30; *Fig.* 14
Borthagaray, Juan M., 109
  Ollé Perez house (Punta Ballena,
    Ur.), 109; *Fig.* 118
Brando, Carlos, 41
  Cerro Piloto housing development
    (Caracas), 41, 43; *Fig.* 26
  El Paraiso housing development
    (Caracas), 41, 43
23 de Enero housing development
    (Caracas), 41, 43; *Figs.* 24–25
Brasilia, Brazil, 27, 35–41, 96, 99
  Civic axis, 36–37; *Fig.* 21
  Development Palace (Niemeyer), 96
  Kubitschek rehabilitation
    center (Campelo), 96
  Plan (Costa and Niemeyer), 36;
    Fig. 20
  Planalto Palace, 37–38; *Fig.* 22
  Plaza of the Three Powers, 37;
    Fig 22
  Supercuadra (residential unit),
    39–40; *Fig.* 23
Bratke, Osvaldo Arthur, 26
Brazil, 13–16, 19–20, 22–27, 30–32,
  35–36, 41, 96, 99, 100, 102, 112,
  114; *Figs.* 6–7, 9–10, 20–23,
  103–110
Bresciani, Carlos, 46, 93
  Portales neighborhood unit
    (Santiago), 46, 48; *Figs.* 27–31
Brother Gabriel, 87
  Benedictine Monastery Church
    (Las Condes, Chile), 87; *Figs.*
    90–93
Brother Martín, 87

Benedictine Monastery Church
(Las Condes, Chile), 87; *Figs.*
90–93
Bullrich, Alicia Cazzaniga de, 116
National Library (Buenos Aires),
116–117; *Fig.* 125
Bullrich, Francisco, 116
National Library (Buenos Aires),
116–117; *Fig.* 125
Burle Marx, Roberto, 22, 26–27
Botanical Gardens (São Paulo), 27
Gardens of Mrs. Odette Monteiro
(Rio de Janeiro), 26–27; *Fig.* 10
Gloria-Flamingo Aterro (Rio de
Janeiro), 27
Parque del Este (Caracas), 27
Plaza (Recife), 22

Calder, Alexander, 73
Campelo, Glauco, 94
S. Kubitschek rehabilitation center
(Brasilia), 96
Canada (Expo '67), 70, 73, 112; *Figs.*
66–70
Candela, Felix, 29, 55, 59, 62, 93
Bacardi bottling plant (Cuatitlán,
Mexico), *Figs.* 45–46
Iglesia de la Medalla Milagrosa
(Mexico City), *Fig.* 50
Iglesia de Neustra Señora de la
Soledad (Coyoacán, Mexico),
Figs. 47–48
Iglesia San Vicente de Paul
(Mexico City), *Fig.* 49
"Umbrellas" (Mexico), *Fig.* 51
Castillo, Fernando, 46, 93
Portales neighborhood unit
(Santiago), 46, 48; *Figs.* 27–31
Castro, Fidel, 62
Catalanism, 15
Catalano, Eduardo, 30
Municipal Auditorium (Buenos
Aires), 30
Caveri, Claudio, 62, 93, 102
Iglesia Nuestra Señora de Fátima
(Martinez, Arg.), 62, 102; *Figs.*
60–61
Celis Cepero, Carlos, 41
Cerro Piloto housing development
(Caracas), 41, 43; *Fig.* 26
El Paraiso housing development
(Caracas), 41, 43
23 de Enero housing development
(Caracas), 41, 43; *Figs.* 24–25
Centella, Juan, 41
Cerro Piloto housing development
(Caracas), 41, 43; *Fig.* 26
El Paraiso housing development
(Caracas) 41, 43
23 de Enero housing development
(Caracas), 41, 43; *Figs.* 24–25
Cerqueira César, Roberto, 26

Cetto, Max, 19
Chile, 14–15, 46, 48, 83, 86–87; *Figs.*
27–31, 84–93
Christophersen, Alejandro, 15–16
Churriguera family, 18
Colombia, 35, 95; *Figs.* 99–102
Comino, Horacio, 31
Tucuman University campus, 31
Constructivists, 28
Correia Lima, Atilio, 22
Santos Dumont airport building
(Rio de Janeiro), 22
Costa, Lúcio, 16, 19, 22–23, 30, 36,
41
Hostel (Nova Friburgo, Brazil), 23
Hungria Machado House (Rio de
Janeiro), 23
Ministry of Education and Health
(Rio de Janeiro), 19–20, 22; *Fig.*
6
Plan for Brasilia, *Fig.* 20
Cravotto, Oscar, 19
Croce, Plinio, 96
Peugeot office building (Buenos
Aires), 96
Cuba, 62, 67, 70, 93; *Figs.* 52–59,
62–68

Dabinovic, Boris
Bus terminal (La Pampa, Arg.),
106–107; *Fig.* 115
Provincial Government House (La
Pampa, Arg.), 106; *Fig.* 114
Da Costa, M.
Cuban pavilion, Expo '67
(Montreal) 70, 112; *Figs.* 66–68
De Castro Mello, Icaro, 26
De Chirico, Giorgio, 38
De Herrera, Juan, 18
De la Mora, Enrique, 54, 59
Compañia de Seguros Monterrey
building (Mexico City), 54; *Fig.*
38
Iglesia de Nuestra Señora de la
Soledad (Coyoacán, Mexico),
Figs. 47–48
Iglesia San Vicente de Paul
(Mexico City), *Fig.* 49
Del Moral, Enrique, 28
De Mello, J. C., 102
Forum (São Paulo), 102; *Fig.* 110
Dieste, Eladio, 54–55, 93
Church (Atlántida, Ur.), 55; *Figs.*
39–43
T.E.M. shed (Montevideo), 55; *Fig.*
44
Domenech y Montaner, 15
Duhart, Emilio, 83, 86–87, 93
United Nations building (Santiago),
83, 86–87; *Figs.* 84–89
Ellis, Eduardo, 62, 102

Iglesia Nuestra Señora de Fátima (Martinez, Arg.), 62, 102; *Figs.* 60–61
England, 15
Erbin, Jorge, 111
Gonzales Porto bookstore (Buenos Aires), 111–112; *Figs.* 119–120

Fernandez, José, 67
J. A. Echeverria University campus (Havana), 67; *Fig.* 62
Ferro, Sergio, 102
France, 15, 37
Friedman, Yona, 99

Gaido, Augusto
Bus terminal (La Pampa, Arg.), 106–107; *Fig.* 115
Provincial Government House (La Pampa, Arg.), 106; *Fig.* 114
Garatti, Vittorio, 62, 67, 70, 93
Ballet School (Havana), 62; *Figs.* 56–58
Cuban pavilion, Expo '67 (Montreal) 70, 112; *Figs.* 66–68
Music School (Havana), 62; *Fig.* 59
Technological Soil and Fertilizing Institute (Güines, Cuba), 70; *Figs.* 64–65
García Nuñez, Julián, 15
Hospital Español (Buenos Aires), 15; *Figs.* 1–2
Gasperini, Gian Carlo, 96
Peugeot office building (Buenos Aires), 96
Gaudí, Antonio, 15, 18
Giorgi, Bruno, 37
"The Warriors" (Brasilia), 37; *Fig.* 22
Gonzalez Pozo, Fernando
Compañia de Seguros Monterrey building (Mexico City), 54; *Fig.* 38
Guedes, Joaquim, 96, 99–100, 102, 114
Breyton house (Sáo Paulo), 102
Colegio Salesiano São José (São Paulo), 102
Costa Neto house (São Paulo), 102; *Fig.* 109
Cunha Lima house (Sáo Paulo), 100, 112, 114; *Fig.* 105
Escola Salesiana (São Paulo), 102
Forum (São Paulo), 102; *Fig.* 110
Landi house (São Paulo), 100; *Figs.* 106–107
Pereira house (São Paulo), 102; *Fig.* 108
Toledo house (São Paulo), 96; *Figs.* 103–104
Güines, Cuba
Technical Soil and Fertilizing

Institute (Garatti), 70; *Figs.* 64–65

Hardoy, Jorge Ferrari, 30
Apartment house (Buenos Aires), 30; *Fig.* 15
Huidobro, Carlos G., 46, 93
Portales neighborhood unit (Santiago), 46, 48; *Figs.* 27–31

Junta Nacional de la Vivienda de Peru, 43–44

Kahn, Louis, 93
Kubitschek, Juscelino, 36
Kurchan, Juan, 30
Apartment house (Buenos Aires), 30; *Fig.* 15

Laurens, Henri, 77
Le Corbusier, 22–24, 28, 30–31, 35, 49, 87, 90, 93–94, 96, 99
Cherchell project (North Africa), 30
Ministry of Education and Health (Rio de Janeiro), 19–20, 22; *Fig.* 6
Petite Maison de Weekend (Boulogne), 30
Ville Radieuse, 35
Lefèvre, Rodrigo, 102
Léger, Fernand, 77
Lestard, J., 111
Gonzales Porto bookstore (Buenos Aires), 111–112; *Figs.* 119–120
Levi, Rino, 26
Loos, Adolf, 49
Lynn, Jack, 46

Manaure, Mateo, 77
Mariscal, Federico, 15
Palacio de Bellas Artes (Meixco City), 15
Martinez de Velazco, Juan
Main library, Ciudad Universitaria (Mexico City), *Fig.* 11
Martorell, José, 94
Mexico, 13–15, 17, 19–20, 28–29, 31–32, 54; *Figs.* 11–12, 38, 45–51
Mies van der Rohe, Ludwig, 32, 96, 99, 109
Mijares, José, 41
Cerro Piloto housing development (Caracas), 41, 43; *Fig.* 26
El Paraiso housing development (Caracas), 41, 43
23 de Enero housing development (Caracas), 41, 43; *Figs.* 24–25
Mindlin, Henrique, 26
Molinos, Oscar, 102
Soldatti house (Martinez, Arg.), 102; *Fig.* 112

Mondrian, Piet, 28

Navarro, 77
Newman, Robert B., 77
Niemeyer, Oscar, 22, 24, 40, 96, 99
  Casa do Baile (Pampulha, Braz.),
    24; *Fig. 7*
Development Palace (Brasilia), 96
  Hospital Sul America (Rio de
    Janeiro), 24
  Hotel Copan (São Paulo), 24
  House (Canoas, Braz.), 24
  Ministry of Education and Health
    (Rio de Janeiro), 19–20, 22; *Fig.*
    6
  Museum of Modern Art (Caracas),
    24; *Fig. 8*
  Petrópolis residential blocks, 24
  Plan for Brasilia, *Fig. 20*
  Yacht Club (Pampulha, Braz.), 24

O'Gorman, Juan, 19, 28–29
  Architect's house (San Angel,
    Mexico), 29; *Fig. 12*
  House (Villa Obregón, Mexico), 19
  Main library, Ciudad Universitaria
    (Mexico City), 28–29; *Fig. 11*
Orozco, José Clemente, 28

Payssé Reyes, Mario, 90
  Banco de la República (Punta del
    Estre, Ur.), 90; *Fig. 98*
  Private house (Carrasco, Ur.), 90;
    Fig. 97
Penteado, H., 102
  Forum (São Paulo), 102; *Fig. 110*
Peralta Ramos, Federico, 49
  Bank of London and South
    America, Harrod's branch
    (Buenos Aires), 107, 112; *Figs.*
    116–117
  Bank of London and South
    America, headquarters (Buenos
    Aires), 49, 51–52, 54, 112; *Figs.*
    32–37
Peru, 13–14, 43–44
Pevsner, Nikolaus, 111
Philip II, 14
Pop Art, 111
Porro, Ricardo, 62, 93
  Modern Dance School (Havana),
    Fig. 55
  Plastic Arts School (Havana), 62;
    Figs. 52–54
Portinari, Candido, 22–23
Prebisch, Alberto, 19

Reidy, Eduardo Affonso, 22, 24, 99
Rey Pastor, José, 102
  Black Beauty horse farm
    (Ituzaingo, Arg.), 102; *Fig. 111*
Richards, J. M., 62

Riegl, Alois, 18
Rietveld, Gerrit Thomas, 102
  Schroeder house (Utrecht), 102
Rivera, Diego, 28
Roberto, Marcelo, 24
  A.B.I. building (Rio de Janeiro), 24
  National Insurance Institute
    building (Rio de Janeiro), 24
Roberto, Milton, 24
  A.B.I. building (Rio de Janeiro), 24
  National Insurance Institute
    building (Rio de Janeiro), 24
Rossi, Francisco
  Bus terminal (La Pampa, Arg.),
    106–107; *Fig. 115*
  Provincial Government House (La
    Pampa, Arg.), 106; *Fig. 114*

Saavedra, Gustavo
  Main library, Ciudad Universitaria
    (Mexico City), *Fig. 11*
Sacriste, Eduardo, 30
  Tucuman University campus, 31
Salinas, Fernando, 67, 93
  Manicaragua housing development
    (Las Villas, Cuba), 67; *Fig. 63*
Salmona, Rogelio, 93
  Marulandia housing development
    (Bogotá), 94–96, 112; *Figs.*
    99–102
Sanchez Elía, Santiago, 49
  Bank of London and South
    America, Harrod's branch
    (Buenos Aires), 107, 112; *Figs.*
    116–117
  Bank of London and South
    America, headquarters (Buenos
    Aires), 49, 51–52, 54, 112; *Figs.*
    32–37
Saurez, Eduardo, 96
  Peugeot office building (Buenos
    Aires), 96
S.E.P.R.A., 49
  Bank of London and South
    America, Harrod's branch
    (Buenos Aires), 107, 112; *Figs.*
    116–117
  Bank of London and South
    America, headquarters (Buenos
    Aires), 49, 51–52, 54, 112; *Figs.*
    32–37
Sert, José Luis, 35
  Cidade dos Motors plans (Brazil),
    35
Siqueiros, Alfaro David, 28
Solsona, Justo, 12, 114, 116
  Banco Municipal (Buenos Aires),
    112, 114; *Figs. 121–122*
  FATE building (Buenos Aires), 116;
    Fig. 124
  National Library project (Buenos
    Aires), 116

Sierchuck house (Buenos Aires), 114, 116; *Fig.* 123
Spain, 14–15
Studer, Edwin, 90

Testa, Clorindo, 49, 93, 106–107, 116
Bank of London and South America, Harrod's branch (Buenos Aires), 107, 112; *Figs.* 116–117
Bank of London and South America, headquarters (Buenos Aires), 49, 51–52, 54, 107, 112; *Figs.* 32–37
Bus terminal (La Pampa, Arg.), 106–107; *Fig.* 115
National Library (Buenos Aires), 116–117; *Fig.* 125
Provincial Government House (La Pampa, Arg.), 106; *Fig.* 114
Tomé, Narcisco, 14
Trasparente, 14
Torres García, Joaquín, 90
Turner, John, 4

Uruguay, 14–15, 19–21, 30, 54–55, 90, 109; *Figs.* 3–5, 13–14, 39–44, 94–98, 118

Valdés, Hector, 46, 93
Portales neighborhood unit (Santiago), 46, 48; *Figs.* 27–31
Varas, A., 111
Gonzales Porto bookstore (Buenos Aires), 111–112; *Figs.* 119–120
Vasarely, Victor, 77
Velazquez, Diego, 18
Venezuela, 13, 20, 24, 27, 41, 43, 73, 77, 81–82; *Figs.* 8, 24–26, 69–83
Vieco, Hernan, 93
Marulandia housing development (Bogotá), 94–96, 112; *Figs.* 99–102
Vilamajó, Julio, 19–21, 90
Facultad de Ingenieria (Montevideo), *Fig.* 3
Private house (Montevideo), 19; *Fig.* 4

Ventorrillo (Minas, Ur.), 21; *Fig.* 5
Vilar, A. U., 19
Villagrán García, José, 17, 19, 28
House (Mexico City), 19
Villanueva, Carlos Raúl, 20, 41, 73–82, 93
Aula Magna, Ciudad Universitaria (Caracas), 73, 77; *Figs.* 75–80
Cerro Piloto housing development (Caracas), 41, 43; *Fig.* 26
Ciudad Universitaria (Caracas), 73; *Figs.* 73–74
El Paraiso housing development (Caracas), 41, 43
El Silencio (Caracas), 73; *Fig.* 71
Museo de Bellas Artes (Caracas), 73; *Fig.* 72
School of Architecture, Ciudad Universitaria (Caracas), 73, 77, 81–82; *Figs.* 81–83
Venezuelan pavilion, Expo '67 (Montreal), 73; *Figs.* 69–70
23 de Enero housing development (Caracas), 41, 43; *Figs.* 24–25
Vital, Alvaro, 19
Vivanco, Jorge, 30
Tucuman University campus, 31
Voluntad y Accion, 30

Warchavchik, Gregori, 19
House (São Paulo), 19
Wells, H. G., 36
Wiener, Paul Lester, 35
Cidade dos Motores plans (Brazil), 35
Williams, Amancio, 31–32, 54
Airport (Rio de la Plata, Arg.), 32
Auditorium (Hall for Plastic Spectacle and Sound), 32; *Fig.* 18
Private house (Mar del Plata, Arg.), 32; *Figs.* 16–17
Suspended office building, 32, 54; *Fig.* 19
Worringer, Wilhelm, 18, 28

Yañez, Legorreta, 28

SOURCES OF ILLUSTRATIONS

Where possible, all sources have been identified.

G. Angulo, Bogotá: 99–101
Arquitectos Americanos Contemporaneos, VII (Buenòs Aires, 1962): 29
Avca, Santiago: 90–93
Horacio Baliero: 113
Juan M. Borthagaray: 118
Francisco Bullrich: 1, 2
Félix Candela: 45, 46
Max Cetto, Villa Obregon, Mexico: 11, 12
Luc Chessex, Lausanne: 53, 55–59, 62
Alvarez Colombo, Buenos Aires: 117, 119, 120
E. Colombo, Buenos Aires: 32–37, 116
Colorfoto, Montevideo: 5
René Combeau, Santiago: 27, 28
Csillag, Santiago: 84
Eladio Dieste: 39–44
Emilio Duhart: 85, 86
Graziano Gasparini, Caracas: 26
Paolo Gasparini, Caracas: 25, 52, 54, 69, 70, 72, 75–77, 80–82
Marcel Gautherot, Rio de Janeiro: 6, 7, 9, 10, 21–23
Henry-Russell Hitchcock, *Latin American Architecture Since 1945* (New
      York: The Museum of Modern Art, 1955): 17
Migone Izquierdo, Buenos Aires: 121, 122
Katzenstein, Buenos Aires: 3, 4
J. M. LePley, Buenos Aires: 112
Ministerio da Construcciones, Havana: 63
Sibyl Moholy-Nagy: 24, 74
Sibyl Moholy-Nagy, *Carlos Raúl Villanueva and the Architecture of Venezuela*
      (New York: Frederick A. Praeger, 1964): 78, 79, 83
V. Moscardi, São Paulo: 105
Stamo Papadaky, *Oscar Niemeyer: Works in Progress* (New York: Reinhold,
      1956): 8
Gomez Piñeiro, Buenos Aires: 15, 60, 61, 125
Rays, Santiago: 87, 88
J. M. Richards: 66–68
Rogelio Salmona: 102
Sansó, Buenos Aires: 94–98
Justo Solsona: 123
Willy Stäubli, *Brasilia* (New York: Universe Books, 1965): 20
Grete Stern, Buenos Aires: 16
Torrente, Santiago: 89
Xavier, São Paulo: 109, 110
Guillermo Zamora, Mexico City: 38, 47–50